The Fall of the Roman Republic

IN THE SAME SERIES

General Editors: Eric J. Evans and P.D. King

Lynn Abrams	Bismarck and the German Empire 1871–1918
David Arnold	The Age of Discovery 1400–1600
A.L. Beier	The Problem of the Poor in Tudor and Early Stuart England
Martin Blinkhorn	Democracy and Civil War in Spain 1931–1939
Martin Blinkhorn	Mussolini and Fascist Italy
Robert M. Bliss	Restoration England 1660–1688
Stephen Constantine	Lloyd George
Stephen Constantine	Social Conditions in Britain 1918–1939
Susan Doran	Elizabeth I and Religion 1558–1603
Christopher Durston	James I
Eric J. Evans	The Great Reform Act of 1832
Eric J. Evans	Political Parties in Britain 1783–1867
Eric J. Evans	Sir Robert Peel
Dick Geary	Hitler and Nazism
John Gooch	The Unification of Italy
Alexander Grant	Henry VII
M.J. Heale	The American Revolution
Ruth Henig	The Origins of the First World War

Ruth Henig	The Origins of the Second World War 1933–1939
Ruth Henig	Versailles and After: Europe 1919–1933
P.D. King	Charlemagne
Stephen J. Lee	Peter the Great
Stephen J. Lee	The Thirty Years War
J.M. MacKenzie	The Partition of Africa 1880–1900
Michael Mullett	Calvin
Michael Mullett	The Counter-Reformation
Michael Mullett	James II and English Politics 1678–1688
Michael Mullett	Luther
Robert Pearce	Attlee's Labour Governments 1945–51
Gordon Phillips	The Rise of the Labour Party 1893–1931
J.H. Shennan	France Before the Revolution
J.H. Shennan	Louis XIV
David Shotter	Augustus Caesar
David Shotter	Tiberius Caesar
Keith J. Stringer	The Reign of Stephen
John K. Walton	Disraeli
John K. Walton	The Second Reform Act
Michael J. Winstanley	Gladstone and the Liberal Party
Michael J. Winstanley	Ireland and the Land Question 1800–1922
Alan Wood	The Origins of the Russian Revolution 1861–1917
Alan Wood	Stalin and Stalinism
Austin Woolrych	England Without a King 1649–1660

LANCASTER PAMPHLETS

The Fall of
the
Roman Republic

David Shotter

London and New York

First published 1994
by Routledge
11 New Fetter Lane, London EC4P 4EE

Simultaneously published in the USA and Canada
by Routledge
29 West 35th Street, New York, NY 10001

Typeset in Bembo by
Ponting–Green Publishing Services, Chesham, Bucks
Printed in Great Britain by
Clays Ltd, St Ives plc

Printed on acid free paper

British Library Cataloguing in Publication Data
A catalogue record for this book is available from the British Library

Library of Congress Cataloging in Publication Data
Shotter, D. C. A. (David Colin Arthur)
The fall of the Roman Republic/David Shotter.
p.   cm. – (Lancaster pamphlets)
Includes bibliographical references.
1. Rome–History–Republic, 265–30 B.C.
I. Title.   II. Series.
DG254.S45   1994
937'.02–dc20   93–44851

ISBN 0–415–10292–8

Contents

List of figures   ix

Foreword   x

Acknowledgements   xi

Introduction: The republic   1

1 The government of the republic   4

2 The growth of empire   10

3 Factionalism in Roman politics:
The Gracchus brothers   17

4 Marius, the army and the Italian allies   29

5 Sulla and the senate   38

6 The domination of Pompey   51

7 The first triumvirate and the slide to civil war   66

8 Caesar's dictatorship   79

9 The final act: Antonius, Octavian and Lepidus   88

Epilogue   96

Appendices

I Roman voting assemblies   101
II Magistracies of the Roman republic   102
III The provinces of the Roman empire   106
IV List of principal dates   108

Further reading   112

Figures

1 Legislation in Rome after 287 BC   8

2 Stemma showing the links between the Scipiones, Claudii and
Sempronii Gracchi   21

3 The Roman empire in AD 14   40

Foreword

Lancaster Pamphlets offer concise and up-to-date accounts of major historical topics, primarily for the help of students preparing for Advanced Level examinations, though they should also be of value to those pursuing introductory courses in universities and other institutions of higher education. Without being all-embracing, their aims are to bring some of the central themes or problems confronting students and teachers into sharper focus than the textbook writer can hope to do; to provide the reader with some of the results of recent research which the textbook may not embody; and to stimulate thought about the whole interpretation of the topic under discussion.

Acknowledgements

My thanks are due to Peter Lee of Lancaster University Archaeological Unit for drawing the map which appears as Figure 3, and to Miss Susan Waddington of the Department of History at Lancaster University for the preparation of the manuscript.

Introduction
The republic

The English word 'republic', derives from the Latin *respublica* – 'the public concern'. Nowadays, when we apply the word to a modern country, we have a specific form of government in mind. Although the Romans continued to use the word to describe their state well into the imperial period, students of Roman history apply it to the state of Rome between the late sixth century BC, when the early monarchy was terminated, and the late first BC, when a new monarchy, which we know as the *principate*, was established by Augustus.

Romans of the *principate* tended to qualify *respublica* with the word *vetus* ('old') when referring to the times before Augustus, and by it they signified a state which lacked the central direction of a monarchic figure, and in which the functions of government were, however nominally, split between three elements – the magistrates (particularly the consuls), the senate (or 'assembly' of the aristocracy), and the people (*populus*) and plebeians in their assemblies – the three *comitia* and the *concilium plebis* (see Appendices I and II). In the eyes of at least one ancient historian, the Greek Polybius, writing in the middle of the second century BC, this 'sharing' of power in a 'mixed constitution' guaranteed stability by ensuring that none of the three elements of government had sufficient power to dominate, and that each depended upon the other two for the discharge of its functions.

1

In truth, Polybius' analysis had more to do with classical political philosophy, as expounded by Plato and Aristotle, than it did with the political realities of Rome. For whilst sovereignty nominally belonged to the people in their assemblies, various factors – economic, political, military and religious – ensured that the people deferred to their 'betters', the leaders of the nobility who, in fact, controlled all aspects of life and government through the senate and the magistracies. Because no salaries were paid for governmental duties, these tasks could in practice be exercised only by the wealthy. Further, because the Roman state made no distinction between civilian and military leadership, these same people held a monopoly of military command. Religion, too – a potent feature in the life of a superstitious people – was under the control of the wealthy who alone had the resources to defray the expenses involved in a complicated, and thus costly, area of Roman life.

As significant, however, was the institution of clientage in which the more fortunate members of society 'protected' those less well-off in return for the latter's political loyalty. Thus a state that had all the political institutions to allow a development into democracy remained unquestionably oligarchic in character.

Superficially, the stability and harmony assumed by Polybius to be Rome's contribution to the development of classical city-states seemed real enough. In fact, it was the temporary product of the period when Rome was fighting first for her survival in Italy and then for supremacy over her Italian neighbours. However, security within Italy brought contacts with people further afield, such as Carthaginians and Greeks, wherein lay both opportunities and dangers.

Warfare imposed strains upon the Roman state by increasing demands upon Roman citizens, but also by bringing obligations and opportunities that individuals could use to their own advantage. Whilst it is commonly (and rightly) argued that the growth of the Roman empire from the third century BC was the general cause of the gradual disintegration and collapse of the republic, it is important to demonstrate the reasons for this, and to show how the old-fashioned 'corporateness' of the Roman state retreated before the surging tide of factionalism and individualism. As a result, the last century of the republic (133–31 BC) was characterised by a series of struggles for

2

military and political dominance fought out by major, often charismatic, figures such as Scipio Aemilianus, the Gracchus brothers, Gaius Marius, Cornelius Sulla, Pompey, Crassus and Caesar, and ultimately by Marcus Antonius and Caesar's adopted son, Octavian, who, as the eventual victor, was to rule the republic and its empire as Augustus Caesar.

1

The government of the republic

The initials SPQR (*senatus populusque Romanus* – 'the senate and people of Rome') encapsulated the theory of the republic's government. In practice, however, as we have seen, the people's exercise of sovereignty was limited, and the aristocracy dominated the government.

Roman society was classified into two groups – patricians and plebeians; the origins of the classification are not known for certain, but in the early republic the patrician aristocracy held a monopoly of power. Over the first two centuries of the republic, changes took place in what is known as the 'struggle of the orders', although the changes were less dramatic than they are sometimes claimed to have been. It is true that plebeians were given access to the magistracies, to membership of the senate and, through their assembly, to sovereignty in the state. However, because the possession of wealth was a prerequisite to effective participation in government, only the richest of the plebeians were in practice able directly to benefit. Thus the chief effect of the 'struggle of the orders' was to widen the aristocracy from patrician alone to include wealthy plebeians, but to leave the vast majority of Roman citizens still with little or no opportunity of making a significant political impact.

There were a number of reasons why the people's sovereignty had little potency. In meetings of the assemblies, the people were under the control of the presiding officer – usually a consul or praetor in the case of the *comitia*, or a tribune of the plebs in the *concilium plebis*; there was neither freedom of debate nor power of initiating business from the floor. The people's function, in other words, was limited essentially to that of voting. Even in this, however, there were major practical restrictions: the principle of 'one man, one vote' did not obtain; the people were divided into groups ('centuries' or 'tribes'), and registered their votes within their groups. A popular decision resulted from achieving a majority of the voting groups. In all of the assemblies, the voting groups were 'rigged' to ensure the predominance of the wealthy. Again, since the principle of the secret ballot was not introduced into assembly business until the second century BC, the people, who were the clients of the rich, were inevitably intimidated in the exercise of their vote by the presence of their aristocratic patrons. To vote against the known wishes of one's patron was a reckless act of disloyalty (*perfidia*), which would likely bring retribution in its wake. Such retribution might consist simply of removing the material benefits of patronage, though since noble patrons at various times in their careers might exercise both civilian and military authority, they were in a position to make life extremely difficult for a recalcitrant client.

In the early republic, the aristocracy were able to exercise a check on popular decision-making through the practice of submitting to the senate bills which had been made law by the people; this was ostensibly to ensure that no legal or religious principles were infringed by any new enactment. Later, it became regular practice, although not a binding requirement, for magistrates to submit their proposals to the senate prior to taking them before the people. In practice, senatorial endorsement in the form of an 'advisory' decree (*senatus consultum*) was considered a necessary prerequisite to the exercise of popular sovereignty. This new procedure, in fact, gave the aristocracy in the senate a stronger hold over the magistrates, and indicates that the popular assemblies were no longer considered a threat. The senate was thought to represent corporately the source of the best political, military, legal and religious wisdom in the republic; its views, once expressed, were lightly disregarded neither by the people nor by individual members of the nobility. It was strengthened in its ability to influence by the fact that the magistrates, no matter how powerful, were elected for one year only, and had to account for their tenure of offices.

The senate was not accountable; it was elected by no one, and met whenever it wished. The only practical check on its members was that in debate junior members deferred to their seniors; the sole control on its membership was exercised originally by the consuls, who would themselves have been to a degree intimidated by the corporate aristocracy. The consuls later delegated this task to two senior ex-consuls who were elected as censors every five years to serve for a period of eighteen months. They saw to it that the membership of the senate consisted of those who had exercised a magistracy, and those who were 'thought worthy' of membership. The censors could also remove unworthy elements. Thus, given the fact that the magistracy could not be regarded as independent of the aristocracy, the senate's membership in essence was self-regulated.

Individual aristocrats clearly valued their membership of the corporate senate. Thus even though they might become extremely powerful during their tenure of the magistracies (especially of the consulship), in practice they were generally disposed to defer to the will of the senate, and should not, therefore, be regarded as independent agents in the process of government.

Although the consuls were the executive officers of the early republic, other offices were created over the years. This largely reflected the growing weight and complexity of state business. The new officers were chiefly thought of as exercising responsibility in specific areas of business (see Appendix II). By the early years of the second century, it was normal for these offices to be held in a particular order (the *cursus honorum*), and minimum ages of tenure and intervals between offices were laid down. This led to the creation of what was in effect a career structure for senators.

Only consuls and praetors enjoyed *imperium*, or executive authority, which enabled them to command armies and preside over the assemblies. In times of severe emergency, this *imperium* could pass to a *dictator*, if both of the consuls agreed to 'abdicate' in favour of such an appointment, which lasted for six months or for the duration of the emergency, whichever was the shorter. It was an indication of the extreme conditions leading to such an appointment that its holders enjoyed immunity to the veto of the tribune of the plebs (see below).

Although, as we have seen, wealthy plebeians were able to benefit from a number of concessions achieved during the 'struggle of the orders', two concessions stand out as particularly important. The first was the achievement, probably in the fourth century BC, of *provocatio*, the citizen's right of appeal to all his peers against the summary imposition of a magistrate's authority. The second, which according to tradition was won early in the struggle (494 BC), was the plebeians' right to elect their own officers – the tribunes ('tribal leaders') of the plebs, of whom there were at first two, but whose number rapidly increased to ten – who presided over meetings of the *concilium plebis*. The decisions of this body (*plebiscita*) bound the plebs and from early times could, if the consuls agreed, be passed through the state's decision-making machinery to become law.

The tribunes were to become extremely significant in the factional in-fighting of the republic's later years; this was largely because of the powers and privileges with which they were early on endowed. These include the tribune's right/duty to interpose his person between those of an 'arresting' magistrate and an 'oppressed' plebeian. This later became a political veto, by which a tribune could halt business anywhere in the political process. The veto was the more potent because of the fact that the tribune's person was inviolable; this put the plebs under a religious obligation to avenge a tribune who had been violated.

In the third century BC the decisions of the plebeian assembly were given the independent force of law. That this did not, however, initiate democracy in the republic was due to a number of factors. First, the tribunes naturally fell into the group of *wealthy* plebians, whose interests were closer to those of the patricians than of their plebeian 'constituents'. Such men had long been able to gain admission to the senate and to the offices of state, and the tribunate, although not properly a magistracy of the whole people, came to be viewed as if it were; thus tribunes were under the same constraints as magistrates to avoid giving offence to powerful men in the senate if they wished their careers to advance.

Second, the plebeian assembly was not a hotbed of revolutionary zeal; it was organised on the basis of the tribes, and its make-up was subject to the same degree of 'rigging' as the other assemblies. In this way, the plebeian assembly could be (and was) organised to reflect the wishes of wealthy plebeians, and thus its 'orthodoxy' was as secure as that of other popular bodies.

Third, the senate's ability to 'vet' legislation was strengthened in the late fourth and early third centuries BC by making much more of an obligation the magistrates' right to seek the senate's view before approaching the people. By virtue of the tribunes' effective position as quasi-magistrates this applied as much to the plebeian assembly as to other popular bodies. Thus the tribunes were drawn in the same way as consuls and praetors into a position where what they presented to the assembly in which they were competent was essentially a senatorial view. The voice of the senate, therefore, dominated those of the magistrates (including the tribunes) and of the popular assemblies (see Figure 1).

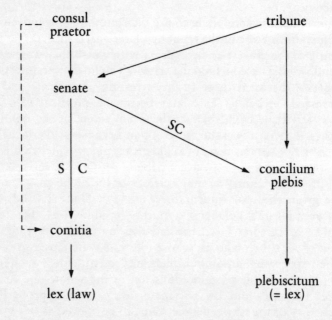

Figure 1 Legislation in Rome after 287 BC
Note: SC = *Senatus Consulto* (By decree of the senate)

The changes of the early republic did not result in the establishment of democracy. The patricians avoided having their self-assumed role in the early republic disfigured by dissonant voices. It is true, of course, that the patriciate itself was, by the third century BC, no longer an exclusive governing elite; rather, its significance had become social. But it had sacrificed only in so far as it had allowed itself to assimilate non-patricians whose views and interests were, in any case, close to its own. The governing class was now made up of patricians and plebeians, within which exclusivity (or 'nobility') was achieved by being able to look back to *consular* ancestors in one's family; members of the governing class thought that membership of the senate and tenure of the magistracies was their birthright. This was their corporate 'freedom' (*libertas*), which was not to be infringed by the over-ambitiousness (*dominatio*) of others.

The Roman noble saw it as his right and duty to serve his country in this paternalistic fashion, and through his service he enhanced his own glory and that of his family. Patriotism and family glory, the twin ambitions of the Roman noble, were also the rocks upon which the republic would founder, as changing circumstances made the latter a more pressing consideration for most than the former. The republic had survived its early tests, but in so doing it had laid the ground which, in the first century BC, would bring it to its knees.

2

The growth of empire

As we have seen, the growth of the Roman empire has been held as the main cause of the breakdown of the old *respublica*. It is important, however, to demonstrate more precisely the nature of the stresses imposed as a result of territorial expansion.

The earliest expansion, not surprisingly, took place within Rome's immediate neighbourhood and was occasioned by a need to acquire more land for its citizens, as well as by a desire to put a 'buffer' between Rome and its enemies. These motives continued to dominate Roman expansion until the middle of the third century BC, by which time she exercised some kind of control or influence over all of Italy south of the river Po.

In these conquests, some land was left with its original owners, but much became the property of Rome ('public land') and was available to be let to locals, to be used for agricultural settlement by Roman citizens, or for the building of towns ('colonies') which were populated by groups of citizens sent from Rome. The attitude of the early republic to its conquered enemies also varied: some might be given full Roman citizenship, though the political privileges of such a grant were in practice usable only in Rome. Others gained 'half-citizenship', which entailed social and economic privileges and protections, though no political rights, except that many were also given the right to settle in Rome and, by so doing, to become full citizens. Others still were given a treaty by which Rome generally

10

DISC GO ROUND

Buy/Trade Form

Date: ___ / ___ / ___   Purchase Invoice # _____

Cust. Name _____

City _____   Zip _____

Phone # _____

DL _____   Birth Date ___ / ___ / ___

Employee Use

___ X ___   ___ X $3.00

___ X $1.00   ___ X $4.00

___ X $2.00   ___ X $5.00

Total CD _____   Total $ Amount _____

Employee _____

circumscribed their ability to act independently. Romans themselves regarded their treatment of Italians as enlightened and pragmatic; it adumbrated the 'civilising mission' which was later to become an important feature of imperial development, and it also created conditions in which, although Italians were actually aiding the defence of Rome, they could also see themselves as part of a united enterprise in which they were linked to Rome by various social and political ties, and in which they joined with Roman citizens as allies in the defence of the common homeland.

There was not a standing, professional army at this stage; that did not come into being until the time of the emperor Augustus. Armies were recruited as and when required, Roman citizens forming the legions and half- and non-citizens amongst the Italians being organised into allied contingents which fought alongside the legions and shared their dangers. Thus men were called away from their occupations; since there was a property qualification for military service, the bulk of the burden naturally fell upon farmers.

This was thought by many to be a desirable situation, as it meant that soldiers had a physical stake in the republic for which they were fighting; in any case, it was thought that the rigours of agricultural life bred the toughest soldiers. Further, the state was left with no problem of settling discharged soldiers when a war was over. This military organisation caused few real problems whilst campaigning seasons were relatively short and wars fought within the confines of Italy, for men could combine farming and military service. However, it did lead to considerable problems as wars gradually became longer and were fought at ever greater distances from Italy.

This mixture of men of different status worked well enough until the second century; then, service conditions for Roman citizens were improved in two ways relative to their non-citizen colleagues. First, in 197 BC, the 'right of appeal' was extended to the citizen on campaign, thus freeing him from his commander's ultimate sanction of summary execution. Second, by a law of 177 BC, Roman citizens were given a greater proportion of war booty. These measures probably reflected a growing disenchantment on the part of Romans towards Italians, and certainly were an important factor in the developing resentment of non-citizens over their treatment by Rome.

11

Some demonstrated their resentment by leaving their homes and settling in Rome – including, it seems, many who were not entitled so to move. Rome's anxiety over this can be seen in the mass expulsions of Italians in 187 and 177 BC, which probably had less to do with 'racism' than with a need to keep men in a position where they could continue to be recruited for military service; for, by leaving their property, such people effectively disqualified themselves from this burden.

In all of this early expansion within Italy there is no indication of any influence by commercial factors; a commercially minded middle class – the so-called equestrian order of Roman society – did not, for the time-being at least, constitute a powerful factor in Roman foreign policy; such people had been effectively squeezed out by the way in which the 'struggle of the orders' had been resolved.

Rome's position in Italy had become that of mistress and protector; it was inevitable that this position would entail obligations as well as opportunities. Indeed, the major wars of the third century BC – against the Samnites, the Carthaginians and the Macedonians – had arisen from problems which bore immediately upon groups of Italians, rather than upon Rome herself. In other words, it can be argued that Rome's entry into the larger world of overseas relations was forced upon her by commitments to her allies, and in no sense was an enterprise undertaken with a positive purpose.

An immediate consequence of this was the acquisition of new territory, with the need to administer it, tax it and, presumably, to exploit it. The initial response in Rome to the problem of provincial government was to elect additional praetors to be responsible solely for the administration of new overseas provinces. Such a solution might have been suitable, had not the number of provinces steadily grown. The consequent prospect of a constant enlarging of the power base, as the number of magistrates required grew, was not welcome to the nobility in Rome. A solution, however, presented itself almost accidentally; Rome's military failures in the early stages of the war against the Carthaginian Hannibal highlighted the need for a continuity of command which the annual changeover of consuls and praetors could not provide. Thus, the senate arranged to prolong a consul's or praetor's *imperium* for a further period; such men were called *proconsuls* and *propraetors*. The senate found such a course of action acceptable because, notionally at least, the person concerned was put under an obligation to the senate for the extension of command.

The principle of prolongation of *imperium* could with little difficulty be extended to the government of the provinces, so that, after holding the consulship or praetorship for a year, a man could be subsequently asked to govern a province for a year as a *proconsul* or *propraetor*. However, whilst this avoided extending the power base too far, it did generate problems of its own. In the first place, whilst a man was consul or praetor in Rome he was in effect 'held in check' by the daily surveillance of his peers, which helped to emphasise the corporate nature of the governing class. In a province, the governor's authority, although *legally* under control, might in effect not be controlled. It is not surprising that some provincial governors should have seen themselves in quasi-regal terms and have been very reluctant to sink back into corporate obscurity when the year of duty was over. Thus, individualism began to prevail over the traditional class loyalties. An early example of the 'risk' was provided by the brilliant but capriciously arrogant Scipio Africanus in the war against Hannibal.

A second problem that manifested itself increasingly in the later second and first centuries BC was the boost which the desirability of winning office gave to electoral corruption; men were prepared to use and borrow huge sums of money to distribute as bribes to the Roman people at election time in the knowledge that they would have the opportunity to recoup their outlay, pay off their debts and make a profit by fleecing provincials.

For many, but particularly for members of the governing class, the growth of the empire opened the opportunity for amassing large sums of money and other material possessions. Such money could be put to work in various ways. The financing of electoral corruption was one form of 'investment'; money could also be put into the acquisition of land, leading to the growth of larger and more efficient agricultural estates, and it could be used to finance major building projects. These not only stood as memorials to those who built them, but they also expanded the facilities available in towns, particularly Rome, thus adding to the attraction of the towns compared with that of the country.

13

This came at a time when farming in Italy was beginning for many to look increasingly unattractive. Much of the war against Hannibal had been fought in Italy; a good deal of agricultural land had been devastated and abandoned by owners and tenants who could not face the prospect of rebuilding their lives. Many such people drifted into Rome and other towns to take advantage of what they had to offer, and, losing their land tenure, disqualified themselves from military service. At the same time, their land was available either to squatters or to those who wished to expand their existing holdings.

Again, although the loyalty of Rome's Italian allies largely stood the test of the pressure exerted by Hannibal's invasion, a few communities were sufficiently exhausted and desperate to have joined Hannibal. This 'disloyalty' exercised a disproportionate influence in Rome, as politicians, perceiving what they took to be the ingratitude of Italians, started to adopt a rather more hostile and arrogant stance towards them, which included, as we have seen, legal provisions which emphasised their inferiority to the citizen legionaries. This deteriorating relationship between Romans and Italians will have driven many of the latter to look for protection by 'usurping' citizenship in Rome itself. It was becoming clear that Roman citizenship for all Italians was becoming an issue in itself which would have to be tackled.

Thus agricultural instability was becoming a major factor in Italy, as people for a variety of reasons deserted the land. Other issues exacerbated these problems; for example, the grain imports which resulted from the tax imposed on the harvested crop in the early provinces could be marketed more cheaply than that which was produced by the Italian farmers. Cheap grain from abroad, of course, also provided a means whereby Roman politicians kept the urban populace under control.

Another result of warfare was an increase in slavery; prisoners of war were brought to Italy to be sold in the slave markets. Many of these people, lacking particular skills, found themselves working on the landed estates of the rich; the almost unlimited availability of such labour permitted the rich a means of farming that was far more 'cost-effective' than was possible for the small farmer. Many of the latter were thus forced out of business, and again had little alternative but to go to Rome in search of work or subsistence.

14

Slavery had a disruptive effect also in the family, the very core of Roman society, which thrived on self-sufficiency, on simplicity and on a clear morality. Thus the tasks that the father and mother performed for the family, including the education of the children, were increasingly handed over to slaves. This dealt a severe blow to the integrity of the Roman family, and many saw it as delivering a death-blow to the fibre of the Roman republic.

The growing empire also provided industrial and commercial opportunities; members of the senatorial order were effectively barred from such activities by a law of 218 BC, presumably to prevent them from deserting the landowning interests that were seen as an essential ingredient of their integrity of character. These opportunities, therefore, fell to others – wealthy men outside the senate who made up the second level of Roman society – the equestrian order. Such men enhanced their wealth, no doubt sometimes acting as 'front-men' for senators, and were able to use it either to enter a public career or to finance the electoral corruption referred to earlier in this chapter.

Further, in the absence of a civil service, the equestrian order was able to use its financial and administrative skills in perform- ing for profit the tasks normally carried out by a civil service, such as tax collection. Groups of equestrians formed themselves into companies to bid for the right to collect taxes, but, of course, collected not just the sum due to be remitted to the treasury, but also their profit as well. In these 'free market' conditions, taxes imposed might bear little relationship to people's ability to pay; in the event of shortfalls, equestrians could act as money-lenders, and could ruin people with the imposition of massive burdens of interest on loans. This was a recipe for instability and disturbance in the provinces which could be used by vigorous enemies of Rome, such as Mithridates of Pontus, to incite rebellions.

The growth of the empire, therefore, presented opportunities and posed problems; the fact that this growth was largely unintended explains why few, if any, contingency plans were made to cope with the problems. The governing class put in place *ad hoc* solutions, and, in its determination to preserve its privileges and vested interests, became narrower in its outlook when it needed to become visionary. As a result, the problems exacerbated each other and overshadowed the benefits of empire.

The family suffered; the Roman governing class, whose strength had for so long resided in its corporate sense, lost this and became embroiled in individual and factional ambition. The small farmer, the backbone of Roman society and the economy, found himself increasingly embattled and incapable of competing, or even of holding his own. A more aggressive attitude to non-citizen Italians destroyed a stability which had taken centuries to develop. Many of those who felt disadvantaged, the objects of discrimination, or simply desperate – citizens and non-citizens alike – came to Rome. The city as a result became a more dangerous and restive place; more important, the loss of such people from their farms meant that a serious difficulty was posed to army recruitment at precisely the time that demands on the army were growing.

A broadly based crisis was fast approaching, though the most immediate manifestation of it lay in the related problems of land tenure and army recruitment. These were the issues upon which individuals and factional groups within the senate were to join in a battle that was to precipitate the fall of the Roman republic.

3

Factionalism in Roman politics
The Gracchus brothers

The senatorial nobility was linked together by ties of family and marriage, but was not by the close of the second Punic War a coherent group; its formerly strong corporate sense had been overtaken by the ambitions of individuals and factional groups. These ambitions, however, tended not to manifest themselves in the formation of 'parties' in a modern sense, offering a choice of policies. Rather, individuals and groups set out to rival each other simply in the amassing of voting clients and thus in their hold on power, whilst their policies could be virtually identical. It is a common error of modern commentators to attach to these factional groups such labels as 'right wing', 'left wing', 're-actionary' and 'progressive'; these terms do not describe the distinctions between Roman groups.

Although many different groups existed, the major ones in the early second century BC were centred around the two leading families – the Scipiones and the Claudii. The chief observable difference between them lay in the grace and culture of the Scipiones, who eagerly embraced the opportunities offered by Rome's new eastern interests, and the narrow nationalism and traditionalism of many of the followers of the Claudii. Such interests were, however, subordinate to the need to live up to ancestral tradition (*mos maiorum*) in the acquisition and reten-tion of power.

The early years of the second century BC saw the dominance

17

of the Scipiones, fresh from Africanus' triumph over Hannibal in 202 BC. Gradually, however, this dominance was eroded, and by the mid-180s BC the Scipionic faction had yielded pride of place to one led by Gaius Claudius Pulcher, whose chief supporters were the cantankerous Marcus Cato (the Censor) and Tiberius Sempronius Gracchus, the father of the tribunes of 133 and 123 BC. By the 150s BC the pendulum had swung again, and the dominant figure in factional politics was Scipio Aemilianus, adopted grandson of the conqueror of Hannibal; his chief rival was the son of Gaius Claudius, Appius Claudius Pulcher, who became the senate's elder statesman (*princeps senatus*) in 136 BC.

By the middle of the second century BC, many of the problems described in the previous chapter had developed to the point where vigorous attention was required. The most immediately pressing, however, was that in which land tenure and military service were bound together.

The problem of recruitment was particularly acute with the legions. Attempts had been made to paper over the cracks by reducing the level of the property qualification and by lowering the number of men in a legion. But still the levy was bitterly resisted, and legions were being sent into the field short of men and with inadequate training. The drift from the land was also exacerbated by the large numbers of deaths as a result of warfare, and by a falling birth-rate. The time, therefore, had clearly arrived for a more radical solution to be attempted, and in the 140s BC a group centred around Aemilianus proposed a programme to resettle landless citizens. It was blocked – presumably for factional reasons – and dropped. But Rome's poor showing in the 130s BC in the Numantine War in Spain demonstrated just how urgent reform really was.

The man whose name is inextricably linked with the next attempt at reform was Tiberius Sempronius Gracchus, tribune of the plebs in 133 BC, and the son of the Gracchus who had in the earlier part of the century been a close ally of Gaius Claudius. The younger Tiberius Gracchus commenced his senatorial career under the auspices of Aemilianus, an arrangement presumably influenced by Cornelia, the mother of the Gracchus brothers and Aemilianus' adoptive aunt; it was normal practice for the younger members of noble families to be introduced into public life in this way by an influential older relative and did not necessarily imply a close or long-lasting political bond between the two. According to Cicero, himself a great admirer of Aemilianus, it was Gracchus' ruthless quest for personal and family glory, a characteristic inherited from his father, which caused him in 137 BC to sever the connection with Aemilianus and, in Cicero's words, 'to become a revolutionary'.

Tiberius Gracchus' year as tribune (133 BC) was dominated by controversial legislative activity and, ultimately, by a frenzy of bloodshed, which included Gracchus' own murder at the end of the year. Gracchus published an agrarian law (*lex Sempronia agraria*), which he proceeded to put, as was the right of his office, before the plebeian assembly, ignoring the normal practice of consulting the senate. The law proposed to take over public land (*ager publicus*) which was held illegally, and to redistribute it in smallholdings to landless citizens.

Who was holding public land illegally? Undoubtedly large-scale landholders had acquired such land during the second century BC as a result of the agricultural upheavals which have already been described; limits were now proposed for the amount of public land that could be held by such people. It is often argued that Tiberius Gracchus offended these men by his proposal and that, for this reason, he bypassed the senate. A second category – probably a great deal more numerous – consisted of people using the land but with no title to it. It is significant that we are told that large numbers of non-citizens came to Rome to agitate in the wake of the Gracchan proposals – presumably people who stood to lose as a result, since citizens were to be the only beneficiaries of the legislation.

This exclusiveness points to two factors. First, and more obviously, the resettlement of citizens on land would at a stroke enhance the body of manpower available for legionary recruitment. Second, if, as seems likely, Tiberius Gracchus' propaganda presented him as a kind 'Robin Hood' figure, robbing the rich to provide for the poor, then he stood to gain a large element of support amongst the urban plebs, who were the traditional supporters of the Scipiones. It is this latter factor that probably explains the strength of the opposition; although ten years or so previously Aemilianus had apparently proposed a very similar measure, he now vigorously opposed it because it threatened to remove from him a significant element of his traditional clientage – a loss which no Roman noble would bear with equanimity.

19

What are we to make of Gracchus' tactic of avoiding consulting the senate about his proposal? Traditional explanations
have ranged, on the one hand, from the supposition that
Gracchus acted in this way out of a conviction that the landed
gentry would be implacably opposed to such a measure to, on
the other, the rather more tame suggestions that he omitted the
consultation either out of eagerness to get on with the job or
from ignorance (or forgetfulness) of constitutional practice.
Against the first of these we may argue that large land-holders
were not major illicit holders of public land. In any case, those
of them who were plebeians could just as well oppose the bill in
the plebeian assembly. It is also significant that in the chaos in
which Tiberius Gracchus' tribunate terminated, the opportunity
was not taken to repeal the measure. The other explanations of
Tiberius Gracchus' behaviour do not really merit discussion.

It is important to note that Tiberius Gracchus' was not a lone
voice; he was part of a faction, evidently headed by no less a
personage than the *princeps senatus*, Appius Claudius Pulcher,
to whose daughter Tiberius Gracchus was married (see Figure 2).
The faction also contained two eminent lawyers, Quintus Mucius
Scaevola and Publius Licinius Crassus Mucianus, who amongst
other things could have put the tribune straight on constitutional practice. Indeed, the make-up of the faction suggests
strongly that the bypassing of the senate was not an 'accidental
error' but a principal feature of the proceedings. A deliberate
and calculated avoidance of senatorial consultation begins to
put the whole enterprise into a somewhat more sinister light.

Avoidance of the senate emphasised a constitutional link
between the tribunes and the plebeian assembly, which had in
practice been soothed by the almost inevitable practice of
tribunes in seeking a senatorial consultation in the same way
as the regular magistrates. It is probably no exaggeration to
say that the sovereignty of the plebeian assembly would not
have come about if it had been thought that there was a real
danger of tribunes using it to establish themselves as independent law-makers.

In other words, there is reason to believe that a principal
objective of this imposing faction was to dominate Rome
through the relationship between the tribune and the plebeian
assembly. Other factors point in a similar direction. First, the
land commission, which was to be established to administer the

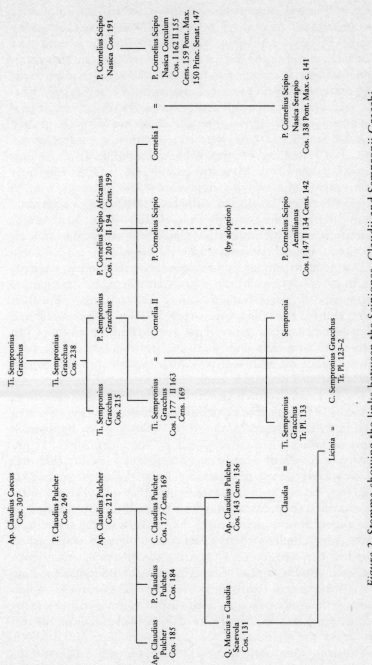

Figure 2 Stemma showing the links between the Scipiones, Claudii and Sempronii Gracchi

proposed resettlement programme, was to be made up of three members of the faction – Tiberius Gracchus himself, his young brother, Gaius, and Appius Claudius. Again, we should note that later in the year Tiberius Gracchus usurped another tradi- tional senatorial right when he sought the authorisation of the plebeian assembly to use a bequest to the Roman people from the late king of Pergamum to finance the resettlement pro- gramme; Gracchus apparently justified his action on the ground that his father had been a patron of the king of Pergamum. Gracchus' handling of opposition also points to a ruthless pursuit of dominance: his fellow tribune, Gaius Octavius, whose family were long-standing supporters of the Scipiones, tried to check Gracchus' legislation with his veto, but was physically removed from the assembly in violation of his legal sacro- sanctity. It is finally evident that Gracchus attempted to seek re- election to the tribunate for 132 BC.

This, to many, amounted to *dominatio*; a faction was attempt- ing to manoeuvre itself into a position where, by 'stealing' its opponents' clientage and controlling an arm of government, it could control Rome in a quasi-regal fashion. The republic had been established to remove regal domination for all time. The actions of Gracchus and his associates amounted to a con- spiracy, made the more sinister in that they tried to hide behind a much-needed piece of reform.

The violence in which Gracchus' tribunate ended, therefore, is hardly surprising; the constitutional violence of the Claudian faction was answered by the overt violence of its opponents. Tiberius Gracchus was murdered by the chief priest, Scipio Nasica, a cousin of Aemilianus. Significantly, we are told that as Nasica left the senate house to perform the deed he pulled his toga over his head – as holders of his office did when perform- ing sacrifice. A political murder was in this way justified as being a sacrifice undertaken in the interests of the republic, a point later emphasised by Aemilianus himself; when asked whether the murder of Gracchus was justified, Aemilianus replied that if the tribune was trying to establish himself as king (*rex*), then he was rightly murdered. Thus the year 133 BC had brought the leading factions into violent opposition and had set a tone of political hooliganism that was to characterise the last century of the republic.

The land bill itself, however, survived, and settlement of

landless citizens proceeded, though at a pace which suggests both that the amount of available land was not great and that this could be only a temporary solution to the original problem – that of legionary recruitment. By 111 BC, in fact, this particular solution had run its course, a fact which, as we shall see, prompted a far more radical course of action on the part of Gaius Marius (see chapter 4).

Attention now turned to the question of franchise for Italians. Gracchus' proposal had probably made matters worse for noncitizen Italians, since many of them had been ejected from public land with no compensation or redress. Large numbers came to Rome to agitate for the granting of full citizenship; their cause was taken up by Aemilianus, who no doubt saw in a successful outcome to this problem a way of recruiting new clientage to replace what he had lost in 133 BC. He did not, however, live to profit from his championing of this cause, for in 129 BC he was murdered; chief amongst the suspects were Marcus Fulvius Flaccus, emerging as the leader of the old Claudian faction, and Gaius Gracchus, younger brother of the tribune of 133 BC.

As this new Gracchan faction took shape, it is significant that it was the issue of franchise for Italians that it promoted, which remained high on the political agenda in the mid-120s BC. In 126 BC, there was a large-scale expulsion of Italians from Rome, and in the next year, following the failure of a relatively modest attempt by Fulvius Flaccus during his consulship to improve the lot of individual Italians, the town of Fregellae (Monte Cassino) revolted and was ruthlessly crushed. It was thus in an atmosphere of crisis that Gaius Gracchus became tribune in 123 BC.

Gaius Gracchus' tribunician legislation is a good deal more complex to consider than that of his brother, since Gaius won a second term as tribune and the chronological relationship of a great many enactments over that period is hard to determine. Nor is there space in the present context to give full treatment to all of the legislation.

It is generally agreed that at an early stage Gaius Gracchus introduced (but subsequently withdrew) a bill to bar from public office anyone who had been deposed from office by the people or plebs. This was obviously aimed at Octavius, his brother's tribunician colleague, and, despite its withdrawal, would have indicated that Gaius did not intend a 'soft' approach to opposition. He also reinforced the principle that the people represented the ultimate source of capital punishment; again, this was aimed particularly at Popilius Laenas, a consul of 132 BC, who had presided at the trials of many of Tiberius' supporters and who was now forced into exile through fear of a retrospective element in the legislation. It was also a warning that Gaius did not intend to fall victim to the same speciously official lynch law by which his brother had been removed.

It is possible that Gaius further consolidated the security of his own position by a corn distribution law (*lex frumentaria*), which offered grain to Roman citizens at a fixed price. Although some accused Gracchus of trying to bribe the populace, it is possible that he was simply looking towards a more equitable distribution of the profits of empire, though in the process it will have done little for Italian farmers trying to make a living by selling their crops. Land resettlement was strengthened by including public land held in the provinces and by undertaking 'multiple resettlement' in the form of new *coloniae* in Italy and abroad.

However, the principal areas touched by Gaius Gracchus' legislation were the future of the equestrian order and the problem of Italian franchise. The equestrians, as we have seen, constituted the second order of Roman society and consisted often of extremely wealthy individuals who preferred a life of business to that of public office and senatorial membership. They were, of course, wealthier and perhaps more politically 'reliable' members of the plebeian assembly than the urban plebs whom Tiberius Gracchus had courted. Gaius appears to have wished to draw a section of the equestrian order into the senate and thus strengthen his position in that body; when this failed he seems to have concentrated on securing for himself the support of these men as well as ensuring that senatorial opponents would not be able to ignore them.

Equestrians were given a stake in the judicial system; for the obvious reason of avoiding corrupt verdicts, they were made the sole source of the jury panel in the court dealing with extortion. It is not clear whether other courts were reformed in the same way, or whether equestrians and senators shared the responsibility of forming the juries for them. A further boost to the businessmen in the equestrian order was given by contracting out the collection of taxes in the newly formed province of Asia, previously the kingdom of Pergamum. Instead of leaving it to local interests to arrange for tax collection, Gaius Gracchus made his contracts the subject of bidding to the censors in Rome by groups of equestrian businessmen who would collect the taxes for private profit. Needless to say, such measures bound these wealthy plebeians to Gracchus' support.

In contrast to his brother, Gaius Gracchus had an interest in the question of Italian franchise; after the death of Aemilianus, Gracchus and Fulvius Flaccus had taken on the Italians' cause, though their progress had not been marked. The revolt of Fregellae, however, emphasised the urgency of the matter; it is thus not surprising that it was the subject of legislation during Gaius Gracchus' tribunate – probably in its second year (122 BC). Although the campaign to clarify the legitimacy of re-election to the tribunate had made little progress, Gaius put himself forward for a second term, and succeeded.

The second term was more troubled than the first, and it is probably significant that Gaius Fannius, one of the consuls of 122 BC, who was an original Gracchan supporter, was certainly not so by the end of the year; there is evidence, too, that Fulvius Flaccus, the most energetic and senior of Gaius' backers, was something of a broken man by the end of 122 BC. The reasons are not difficult to find; the great stream of legislative activity, which should probably be ascribed to the first term, had created much opposition in senatorial circles. Gaius' continuation of his brother's work in land resettlement had had to be slanted differently in order to avoid antagonising Italians by the consequent land confiscations; hence Gracchus' proposals for overseas *coloniae*. To landless citizens in Rome, however, the prospect of settlement overseas would not have been particularly attractive; in addition to this, the 'flagship' *colonia*, Junonia, to be established on the site of Rome's old enemy Carthage, was thought by many to be ill-omened. Thus the continued support of the urban plebs could no longer be taken for granted.

The second year of Gaius' tribunate saw opposition in a more organised form, for his enemies amongst the nobility put their weight behind another of the tribunes of 122 BC, Marcus Livius Drusus. Drusus' chief tactic was not apparently the use of the veto but the proposal of measures to outdo Gracchus on his own ground, and thus to accelerate the erosion of his support. These included a proposal to establish more *coloniae* in Italy. Further, when Gaius brought forward his own franchise proposal – a

25

relatively modest measure to grant full citizenship to half-citizens and half-citizenship to non-citizens – Drusus capped it with a proposal for universal citizenship for Italians.

Gracchus' support amongst the urban plebs was further weakened since the plebs did not wish to share their privileges with 'outsiders'. Moreover, many members of Rome's noble families viewed extension of the franchise with alarm since for them problems would be posed by the assimilation of new citizens into the network of clientage and electoral corruption. Of course, Drusus and his backers in no sense wanted the passage of his proposal; it was merely a tactic to undermine Gaius Gracchus. As such, it succeeded, for Gaius' proposals failed to command support in the plebeian assembly, and Gaius himself failed in his bid for a further term of office in 121 BC. It seems that the opposition to Gaius Gracchus was a good deal more determined, organised and flexible than he appears to have expected.

There is little doubt that the ultimate objective of Gaius Gracchus' opponents was not simply to defeat him but to destroy him completely. The year 121 BC opened with what appears to have been deliberate provocation, led by the anti-Gracchan consul Lucius Opimius; in particular, an attempt to repeal the law establishing the *colonia* of Junonia provoked the Gracchans into street-fighting. Opimius' reaction was to exploit the heightened political tension by making out that the republic was in grave danger. This gave him the opportunity of putting Gracchus' supporters in the senatorial and equestrian orders into a dilemma, since continued support of Gracchus was bound in such an atmosphere to appear tantamount to treason.

A further ominous development, which was to have severe consequences in the ensuing decades, was Opimius' persuasion of the senate to pass what was called the *senatus consultum ultimum* ('the ultimate decree'), which was in effect a declaration of a national emergency, empowering the consuls to do whatever was thought necessary to protect the republic, and was obviously capable of cynical manipulation in the interests of individuals and factions. Besides this, as Julius Caesar was to show in the late 60s BC, it had no basis in law, for no decree of the senate could remove the citizen's right of appeal to the people in capital cases; only a formal meeting of the Roman people could remove this basic right of the Roman citizen.

Little notice, however, was taken of such niceties in the highly charged atmosphere of 121 BC. Opimius put troops into the streets, and the Gracchans stood no chance against them; Fulvius Flaccus was killed, Gaius Gracchus committed suicide, and severe measures were taken against their families. With an ultimate demonstration of cynicism, Opimius, the architect of savagery, erected a temple to *Concordia*.

The Gracchan episode thus ended in violence and bloodshed. What had been demonstrated about the nature and conduct of Roman politics? Clearly, the interests of individuals and factions had come to predominate over the corporate sense that had previously bound the nobility to the interests of the republic. The machinery of government of the republic was wide open to cynical manipulation by pressure groups, and since there was little real difference of view amongst the nobility on many of the major issues, the issues themselves could be used as the factions tried to outdo each other in the quest for clientage and electoral power. A major weapon in this struggle was the use of bribery of one sort or another – either crudely financial or through the passage of measures to benefit any one group within the electorate. Tensions inevitably rose as groups tried to turn temporary factional superiority into a more permanent, and resented, domination.

During the Gracchan period, the position of Italians had scarcely advanced, and a lasting solution had not been found to the problem of military recruitment; the solving of such issues was almost incidental to the ambitions of the political dynasts. Tradition has seen Tiberius Gracchus as the eager and committed reformer and his brother as an embittered soul yearning for vengeance; a cooler estimate might view Tiberius as a cynical manipulator and Gaius as more concerned with coming to grips with the issues of the day.

Finally, two new words had entered the political vocabulary which were to be important in the last century of the republic. First, the Gracchans were rather disparagingly described by their opponents as *populares* ('mob-panderers'), a term referring to their practice of promoting their cause through the manipulation of the popular institutions and at the expense of the senate. The *populares* were not thrusting outsiders; they were an integral part or faction of the nobility. Not surprisingly, their opponents chose a far more honourable word for themselves –

27

optimates ('the best men'). Again, the word does not single them out as aristocrats but indicates their own view that a traditional approach to government, based upon the practical primacy of the senate, represented the best way. In following it, the *optimates* were displaying traditional virtues and acting in a manner consistent with ancestral custom. The politics of the late republic revolved around the *optimates* and *populares*; each contained groups of factions and ambitious individuals whose objectives remained unchanged: the acquisition and use of power.

4

Marius, the army and the Italian allies

The *optimates* emerged from the Gracchan episodes firmly in the ascendant; Opimius was not punished – indeed, he was even supported by at least one prominent ex-Gracchan, Gaius Papirius Carbo. The land legislation was subjected to interference; settlers were allowed – even encouraged – to leave their holdings, whilst those who did not were charged a rental, the proceeds of which were used to finance the corn dole. In addition, further land distribution was halted. The equestrians were confirmed in the gains they had made under Gaius Gracchus' legislation. Thus, the *optimates* set out to ensure the support of those elements of society that had been, temporarily at least, so attached to Gaius Gracchus. Needless to say, no attempt was made to put into effect the more radical of Drusus' 'capping' proposals of 122 BC.

The run of events, moreover, in the years following the death of Gaius Gracchus was to put a solution to the republic's real problems as far away as ever. In particular, the problem of military recruitment remained intractable, even though the empire was continuing to grow, and with it the army's commitments.

Politically, the most significant of these commitments was to be in north Africa, where the senate entered into a war fought not for any territorial gain, but to protect the developing business interests of equestrians against the marauding tactics of

29

the guerilla Jugurtha. The nature of this war was ill-suited to the deployment of standard legionary formations, and its conduct was plagued with dissension and suspected corruption on the part of those members of the nobility sent out to deal with it. Ironically, one of those who came judicially to grief over this was Lucius Opimius, the murderer of Gaius Gracchus; as Cicero was later to observe, Opimius was condemned in a court whose jurors were selected according to the legislation of Gaius Gracchus.

Opimius' condemnation by an equestrian jury is itself indicative of the frustration being felt by the equestrians over Rome's inability to bring the north African war to a successful conclusion; indeed, their financial loss was being compounded by the venality of *optimate* leaders, such as Opimius. Corruption, however, was only a part of the problem; just as damaging were the shortcomings of the army, which served to emphasise the continuing need for reform.

Ironically, the solution to the problem of recruitment came in the wake of the *optimates'* attempt to put into the field a more satisfactory commander, in the hope that, with an end to corruption, the war could be brought to an end. The choice fell upon Quintus Caecilius Metellus, one of the consuls of 109 BC, whose family, although not noted for radical tendencies, had been marginally attached to the Gracchan factions. More pertinently, the Metelli had enjoyed good patronal relationships with members of the equestrian order; indeed, the fact that Metellus was accompanied to Africa by one of his more vigorous clients, Gaius Marius, is proof of this.

The family of Gaius Marius came from the Italian town of Arpinum; although there has occasionally been a tendency to think of Marius as an 'untutored countryman', in fact his family was one of the most thrusting and wealthy in Arpinum and had achieved a leading local status by means of the wealth that had been acquired through mining in Spain. Like many members of the municipal aristocracy, Marius' family had equestrian status, and it was not unusual for young men of Marius' type and status to aspire to putting their feet on at least the lower rungs of the. senatorial *cursus honorum*, though they would not expect to reach the summit of that career in the first generation of achieving senatorial status. Even small success would for such men require the support of a patron from a leading senatorial family. Thus, Marius' achievement in reaching not just one consulship, but seven, before his death in 86 BC, has to be regarded as a truly remarkable demonstration of his single-minded ambition.

Quintus Metellus must have had a far-seeing view of Marius' qualities and their relationship appears to have survived Marius' temerity in putting his patron in jail during his tribunate in 119 BC. Marius held the praetorship in 115 BC and made no secret of his desire to attain the consulship; he soon asked Metellus for leave to return to canvas for the consulship of 107 BC. Metellus, not surprisingly, was discouraging; not only did he realise the normally poor chances of a 'new man' in such an election, but he was aware too that his own reputation as a patron would suffer in the event of Marius' almost inevitable failure. Not unreasonably, he urged Marius, to wait for a more favourable moment; such a delay did not, however, suit Marius, who was already approaching the age of fifty.

So Marius defied Metellus, and won the consulship by appealing to the equestrian order and the urban plebs, both of whom wanted an end to the African war; the basis of Marius' appeal was a pledge to win the war and, if elected, to replace Metellus as commander. Contrary to tradition, he was given the command as the result of a decision of the plebeian assembly. Of course, Marius still had to fulfil his pledge.

This he managed to do by means of a complete reform of the Roman army and its tactics; the tactical changes need not concern us, but Marius' reform of the method of recruitment was to have far-reaching implications for the late republic. The property qualification for legionary service was removed and recruitment was opened to all citizens, regardless of status. Whilst this solved the long-standing problem of recruitment, it failed to address a major consequence. Previously, the state had not needed to take on any particular responsibility for its soldiers when their duty was complete, since the farmer-soldiers returned to their land. But by definition, many of the new recruits had nothing to which to return. Many, therefore, preferred to serve under a successful commander who could lead his army to enormous rewards in the form of booty. Second, the state made no provision, as Augustus was to make later, for the automatic distribution of land to discharged legionaries; rather, on each occasion on which an army returned to Italy for

31

demobilisation, its general had to arrange for the passage through the senate and people of an agrarian law to acquire and provide the necessary land. Events were to show, particularly in Pompey's case in the late 60s BC, that such legislation could become ensnared in factional rivalry and delayed indefinitely. These factors emphasised the close interrelationship between an army commander and his troops, and effectively turned the legionaries into their generals' clients, who felt an obligation to do whatever was asked of them if it appeared to be to their mutual advantage. Events were to show that this might include furthering a general's ambitions by threatening the republic with civil war.

For the moment, however, the horizon was not clouded by such thoughts; there were problems of a different nature. Marius defeated Jugurtha, but closer to home loomed a danger posed in western and southern Europe by the movements of two north German tribes, the Cimbri and Teutones. These movements, which brought the tribesmen in search of new homes first into southern France and then into northern Italy, were a symptom of a much longer-term population instability in the central part of Europe. This instability applied a westward pressure on to tribes living close to the Rhine, and was to be repeated in a different form just over half a century later when Julius Caesar was sent to Gaul to drive the Helvetii back into Switzerland and King Ariovistus of the tribe of the Suebi back across the Rhine. Immediately, however, a series of consular commanders between 113 and 105 BC was unable to halt the Germans.

In this dangerous atmosphere there was a general agreement that Marius was the only man who could save Rome and Italy. In defiance of the law (*lex annalis*) of 180 BC, which laid down intervals between tenures of the same office, Marius was elected as consul for 104 BC. Again, he was successful in handling the military threat, though helped by somewhat aimless tactics on the part of the Cimbri and Teutones. He was then re-elected to the consulship each year until 100 BC, and in two significant battles – at Aix-en-Provence in 102 BC and at Vercellae (near Milan) the following year – he removed the German threat for the moment at least. Marius' consulships of 103–101 BC represented a juncture of support between equestrians and ordinary voters, but probably did not please *optimates*, since it was the shortcomings of some of their number that Marius was having to rectify. The sixth consulship (in 100 BC), however, appears to have stemmed from a universal desire to acknowledge what was owed to Marius for his courage and skill in organisation.

If Marius trod the path of a hero in Rome's military affairs, his position in domestic politics was a good deal more tenuous. His own background led to significant expectations of his government on the part of Italians and equestrians. But these were not to be fulfilled; not only was there a limit to what Marius could achieve, but also even his inclination is open to question.

As a 'new man' in politics, he would have been made to feel that the nobility had granted him the concession of entry for which he should feel obligation. A 'new man' had no obvious place in the oligarchic clique and no natural area of powerful clientage. Thus, like Cicero forty years later, Marius inevitably experienced a continuing dependency which, except in the military sphere, denied him the kind of influence which would normally be associated with a *consularis* (ex-consul) of his standing. Also, it might normally be expected that, as an outsider, he would have attached himself to populist causes; that was not, however, Marius' inclination. Rather, he was a traditionalist at heart and wanted above all to be accepted in the circles of the oligarchic *nobiles*. Thus, divorced from the company of his army, he remained essentially a cipher in politics, with the result that, instead of being a manipulator, he suffered from the manipulations of others; he was forced into the arms of those politicians who needed him enough to associate with him. In all likelihood, it was Marius' frustrated ambition to be an accepted *optimate* that led to the inauguration of an episode of frenzied butchery in Rome shortly before his death in 86 BC.

In Marius' case, the unscrupulous 'minders and manipulators' were Lucius Appuleius Saturninus and Gaius Servilius Glaucia. A *coup d'état* was the last thing on the mind of Gaius Marius, but Saturninus and Glaucia, sharper perhaps than Marius, had seen the potential of Marius' veterans to help them prosecute their vendetta against the *optimates*, particularly Marius' former patron, Metellus Numidicus, who, as censor in 102 BC, had downgraded both of them.

Saturninus and Glaucia were *populares* after the manner of Tiberius Gracchus and with ruthless opportunism exploited issues for their own advancement. As tribune for a second time in 100 BC – though only because of the murder of one of the successful candidates – Saturninus followed the Gracchan example, ignored the senate and took his legislative programme to the plebeian assembly. Marius, as consul, and Glaucia, as praetor, connived at this – not surprisingly, on Marius' part, since Saturninus' *lex agraria* included the provision of land for Marius' veterans. Land in northern Italy was taken from its rightful owners to be included in a programme of distribution to Roman citizens; added to this, the plight of small farmers was made even worse by a further lowering of the grain price in the proposal for a new corn law. Senators were required to swear an oath to uphold Saturninus' laws; all except Numidicus complied. A tribune who tried to exercise his veto was treated as Octavius had been by Tiberius Gracchus.

Not surprisingly, the atmosphere was fraught, with open violence erupting on the streets. Further echoes of a Gracchan-style 'monarchy' emerged in the plans for the election of Glaucia as consul for 99 BC (for which he was not qualified under the *lex annalis*) and for the re-election of Saturninus as tribune. In the violence, another consular candidate, Gaius Memmius, well respected as a man of moderation, and, importantly, a patron of equestrian businessmen, was murdered. None of this would have been welcome to Marius, but he was in the unenviable position of having seriously divided loyalties, particularly when, to respond to the violence, senators armed their own retainers and, as in 121 BC, passed the *senatus consultum ultimum*.

Marius was in an impossible position for, although the 'ultimate decree', as we have seen, carried no legal weight, it called upon the consuls to defend the state. To do so, however, required Marius to attack his allies, and disloyalty (*perfidia*), whatever its context, was intolerable. In so far as he reached a decision over his dilemma, Marius appears to have tried to protect his friends, but they were in any case stoned to death by a mob, despite the fact that the person of Saturninus at least, as tribune, was sacrosanct.

The fiasco meant the eclipse of an embittered Marius; his background put him outside the factions of the *optimates* and *populares* except when he could be useful to either of them, and in this marginalised position he could not fail to offend. To his failure as a factional politician we must add that his dalliance with Saturninus and Glaucia led to his being identified as anti-

Italian (because of Saturninus' land allotments) and anti-equestrian (because of Memmius' murder). Effectively, though not intentionally perhaps, the *nobiles* had destroyed the *novus homo*. The legacy of Marius was even more damaging: an army which could win foreign wars but which was vulnerable to political manipulation; the reinforcement of violence as a normal feature of the political armoury; the disappointment of the equestrians; and, finally, the frustration of the Italians, whose ambitions for citizenship seemed as far from fulfilment as ever. This was a mixture with an extremely explosive potential.

For the time being, the *populares nobiles* had overreached themselves. The 90s BC saw the equestrian order temporarily and uneasily allied to the *optimates*, but the equilibrium was fragile, and based upon largely negative factors. In particular, pressures developed from the dissatisfactions and anxieties of Italians. Relationships between *optimates* and equestrians worsened, largely over the corruption evident in a number of decisions handed down by the extortion court, which was controlled by equestrians. Towards the end of the decade emerged a figure who has been seen as a forlorn voice of conciliation.

This was Marcus Livius Drusus, the son – or, possibly, the nephew – of the Drusus who opposed Gaius Gracchus in 122 BC; Drusus was elected as tribune for 91 BC. His main proposals consisted of a reform of the senate's membership to include a considerable number of equestrians, together with a return of control of the jury panels to senators. At the same time, Drusus included proposals concerning land distribution and corn doles that were reminiscent of activity by *populares* since the Gracchi. Finally, Drusus proposed to enrol in the franchise all Italians living south of the river Po.

Because Drusus was murdered soon after making his proposals, it is hard now to be certain of his aims and motives. He may have been a moderate man, a conciliator who, in the event, found it impossible to draw all groups to support him. Alternatively, the motives may have been more cynical, particularly in view of his father's behaviour in 122 BC. He may have hoped to keep the *populares* at bay by 'stealing their clothes'; there was much in Drusus' programme that had figured in the proposals of the Gracchi. It should also be noted that an enhanced senate would inevitably have undermined the direct relationship between legislator and voters that was a hallmark of the activities of the *populares*.

In one respect, however, the murder of Drusus was a crucial event; whatever the real motives behind the legislation, Italians evidently believed that the proposals of Drusus represented their best chance of securing the objective of citizenship. His death appeared to leave the goal as far away as ever, and resentment burst forth with the open war that had been threatening to erupt since the middle of the second century BC. The Social War (91–88 BC) demonstrated that the Italians could give Rome a military shock but ultimately had little chance of achieving a victory. For their part, the Romans won the war but had evidently learned enough to concede the issue on which it was fought.

On the Italian side there were various motives at work in the war: some wished to create an Italian state independent of Rome, whilst others wanted independence, but in alliance with Rome. Some wanted simply the protection that citizenship would bring, whilst others, particularly in the north of Italy and at the greatest distance from Rome, realised that, with Rome as effectively the only place where the rights of citizenship could be exercised, the achievement of citizenship might in fact make little difference. Those with latin rights (half-citizenship) had no interest in the struggle, and the *coloniae* in various parts of Italy remained loyal to Rome, in effect creating diversions that prevented the Italians from deploying their troops as single-mindedly as they might have wished. Only a few fought out of genuine hatred of Rome, and these were mainly Rome's old enemies in the interior of southern Italy, who not only held out longer than the rest but also made contact with Rome's most serious external enemy of this period, Mithridates, the king of Pontus in Asia Minor.

The *lex Plautia-Papiria* and the *lex Pompeia* of 89 BC represented the formal end of the struggle – the former granting full citizenship to all Italians living south of the river Po, the latter, the proposal of Pompey's father, a consul of 89 BC, granting half-citizenship to the Transpadanes of Cisalpine Gaul. With the concession of the citizenship issue, a new concept was born – *tota Italia* ('Italy united') – which was to play an increasingly important part in the politics of the late republic, and became one of the more potent slogans of the emperor Augustus. The centre of the empire was now not so much 'Rome' as 'Rome and Italy', and imperial policy needed to take account of this expanded homeland.

5

Sulla and the senate

The Social War masked, temporarily, some of Rome's political problems and created some of its own. As soon as the war was over, factional and individual rivalry, which had been the essence of political activity since the middle of the second century BC, re-emerged to thrive on current issues.

The central issue remained the nature of the government of the republic. Was it, as the *optimates* believed, to be the preserve of the nobility and based upon the deliberations of the senate and the vote of the *comitia*? Or should the view of the *populares* prevail that government was the business of the magistrates, and particularly the tribunes, dealing directly with the *comitia* or the plebeian assembly? Even more than previously we become aware that in the last half-century of the republic the *optimates* and *populares* did not comprise monolithic parties with programmes but were broad descriptions of people who might be linked by their views on political methodology but who, even within each of the two groups, might entertain great rivalries.

A significant new factor in the question of the nature of the government was the sudden influx of new citizens as a result of the Social War, though it has to be kept in mind that these could exercise their voting power only if they came to Rome. It is doubtful whether many could afford the expense or time to make the journey and, in any case, until the time of Sulla, elections were held at the end of the year when travelling to

Rome would have been even more difficult. Nor was much gained by Sulla's transference of elections to the summer, since at that time many rural voters would have been detained at home by commitments on their farms.

Since the reforms of Marius, the Roman army was a far more effective force for prosecuting foreign wars, but it had also become a much more unpredictable element in Roman politics. The failure of the republic to make automatic provision for the discharge of soldiers made it inevitable that members of the army would effectively be pushed into the patronage of their generals; this was to have disastrous consequences in the light of the republic's continued insistence on vesting civilian and military authority in the same men.

Abroad, the major issue remained the consequences of the haphazard growth and organisation of the empire. In the first quarter of the first century BC the problems were more apparent in the east than in the west. There were at this stage two provinces in Asia Minor – Asia and Cilicia (see Appendix III and Figure 3); surrounding territory was governed by a variety of kings with some of whom Rome had treaty relationships, though these 'client kingdoms' could prove extremely unreliable in times of crisis. In the early first century BC, Mithridates, the king of Pontus, proved to be the kind of dominating figure who could upset any political equilibrium. Mithridates cast himself in the role of the deliverer of the people of Asia Minor from the ravages of their oppressors; in 88 BC, he swept through the province of Asia butchering all Romans in his path. Thus, at the moment the Social War ended, there was an immediate need both to salvage Roman pride and to restore the stability of the area.

Against this troubled background, the warring between the factions of the *optimates* and *populares* erupted anew; it was fuelled by the deep personal rivalry between the ageing and bitter Marius and Lucius Cornelius Sulla, a junior officer (*quaestor*) in Marius' campaign against Jugurtha, but now basking in the glory accorded to a national saviour in the struggle with the Italians. Sulla was an *optimate*, mindful of the interests of his class; as consul for 88 BC, he controlled the senate and the *comitia*. He calmed the fears of many of his fellow nobles by restricting the enrolment of the new citizens to eight of the thirty-five tribes. This was an important, if temporary, victory, since

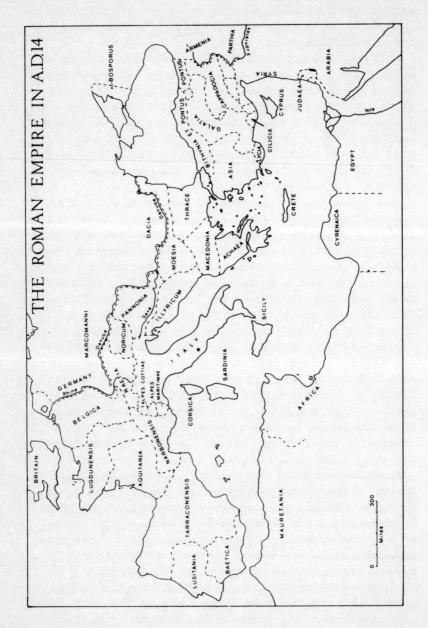

Figure 3 The Roman empire in AD 14

the tribes formed the basis of organisation of both the *comitia tributa* and the plebeian assembly. In the *comitia centuriata*, the organisation of which was based upon wealth, the impact of the new citizens was less marked.

Amongst the *populares*, the most vocal figure was Publius Sulpicius Rufus, one of the tribunes of 88 BC. It is impossible now to reconstruct the real objective of Sulpicius, since he did not survive the year of his tribunate. It is likely, however, that he wanted to achieve the even distribution of the new citizens amongst all of the thirty-five tribes; he may have wanted this out of a sense of justice to the Italians, or he may have seen it as a way of securing his dominance in the plebeian assembly. It is possible that his other measures were subsidiary to this – acting against senators in debt (to please the equestrians) and trans-ferring to Marius the command against Mithridates which the senate and people had recently given to Sulla. The latter measure was illegal and unnecessary.

Sulpicius' legislation was passed amidst scenes of violence in which the tribune protected himself and intimidated others by what amounted to a small private army. The consuls were driven out of Rome. The inevitable sequel was Sulla's reasser-tion of his authority by marching an army against Rome – the realisation of the threat that had lain dormant since Marius' reform of recruitment. Sulpicius' legislation was set aside on the ground of the violence that had been used to pass it; not surprisingly, this provoked a violent reaction in which Sulpicius Rufus, despite the sacrosanctity of his office, was murdered, whilst Marius escaped to north Africa.

Before departing on the Mithridatic command which, of course, was now restored to him, Sulla took the initial steps in what was to be a much more thoroughgoing reform of govern-mental practice in the late 80s BC. To bolster his *optimate* supporters, he enshrined in law the legislative route hallowed by tradition – that is, through the senate and the *comitia centuriata*, the assembly which favoured the *optimates*; this had the effect, of course, of marginalising the power of the tribunate. As a precaution – though, in the event, a vain one – Sulla required his consular successor, Lucius Cornelius Cinna, to swear on oath that he would not tamper with the new arrangements.

Cinna, however, a *popularis* in the manner of Sulpicius Rufus, reintroduced Sulpicius' measure concerning the new citizens and was promptly driven from Rome by his colleague. Cinna retaliated by raising an army in the south and was joined by Marius, who, on his return from Africa, had done likewise in the north. The pair took Rome by force, and Marius and his friends initiated a bloodbath in a desire for vengeance against those whom he believed had wrecked his career from spite. This witch-hunt inevitably created a great desire amongst Sulla's supporters for counter-vengeance. Finally, Cinna and Marius were declared consuls for 86 BC – Cinna's second, and Marius' seventh tenure of the office. The excitement, however, proved too much for the septuagenarian Marius, who died a few days after assuming office.

With little attention to formality, Cinna secured re-election for 85 and 84 BC, choosing his colleagues in each year. Although some useful work was done in these years with economic and monetary reform, and although the new citizens were at last distributed throughout all the tribes, the chief concern was the absent Sulla. Although formally he had been outlawed and exiled there was little chance of giving practical effect to the sentences. Two factors operated in Sulla's favour. First, he seemed able to engineer the downfall of those sent east to deal with him, including Cinna himself who was murdered by his own troops in 84. Second, his campaign against Mithridates was proving successful, for although Mithridates had penetrated as far west as mainland Greece, he was gradually driven back; by 85/4 BC he was once again restricted to Pontus and now recognised as a client and friend of Rome. Sulla re-established the integrity of provinces and kingdoms in the area and wrought a bitter revenge upon all those communities in the province of Asia which, for whatever reason, had had dealings with Mithridates. Many towns were burdened with impossible obligations and, unable to face the demands of Roman tax collectors, were forced into a wretched condition at the hands of equestrian money-lenders.

This first Mithridatic war might have offered a chance for stability had Sulla found time during his active legislative period in 81–80 BC to ratify the arrangement he had made. The failure to do this left Mithridates feeling free to pursue his mischief-making in the area.

By 83 BC Sulla had reached Italy; he was immediately joined by many *nobiles* whose families had suffered at the hands of

Marius and his friends – men such as M. Licinius Crassus, Gnaeus Pompeius (Pompey), and Metellus Pius (the son of Marius' old patron, Numidicus). The progress of Sulla and his associates through Italy was marked by the butchery of political opponents; as in Rome from 82 BC onwards, such behaviour had two objectives – the elimination of political rivals and the acquisition of the funds that would be needed for political bribery and for providing land for his military veterans. By late 82 BC, Sulla had marched an army into Rome for the second time in the decade and taken control. Both consuls had died in the fighting; to fill the gap, Sulla (presumably at his own suggestion) was made *dictator*, the first holder of the office for over a century. This tenure was, however, unlike earlier ones, for the normal tenure of six months was scrapped and Sulla was given leave to hold the office for as long as he thought necessary; in fact, he held it until his sudden and unexpected resignation in 79 BC, and was consul also in 80 BC.

Sulla was of patrician nobility, though his family was not particularly wealthy or politically notable. This may in part explain the personality cult that was encouraged and is demonstrated in not just the high profile of his office, but in the adoption of the name *Felix* ('favoured by the gods'), the erection of an equestrian statue of himself in the forum, and the unprecedented striking of coins bearing his own portrait. In other words – and it was a policy of high risk – he set out visibly to dominate as few, if any, Roman politicians had before him.

The dominance, however, was not achieved simply through propaganda; he had already demonstrated his ruthlessness with his two marches on Rome; once installed in power, he proceeded with the elimination of opponents. This was achieved by a programme of proscriptions, by which a list of 'public enemies' was posted containing the names of men who could be murdered for a reward. The numbers quoted in antiquity of those involved vary from 2,000 to 9,000, the majority of whom were equestrians. There is little doubt that the lists were used by Sulla's henchmen to settle their own scores and that names were added to the lists after the murders had been perpetrated. From Sulla's own point of view, the proscriptions had decided advantages. First, they eliminated opponents and deterred those who might contemplate opposition. Second, since it was rich men who were affected and since the property of a proscribed person was forfeit to the state, the programme provided Sulla with the money he needed for rewards, bribery and providing land for his veterans. Third, he was able to enfranchise the former slaves of the proscribed; as a result, the citizen lists are said to have grown by some 10,000 men, who could be expected to demonstrate their gratitude by giving Sulla their votes in the assemblies.

Such measures might be regarded as preliminaries – the preparation of a ground in which his political reforms might prosper. Sulla was an *optimate* and we might regard his reforms as representing a totally factional approach to the state of the republic. Alternatively, we might, as some have done, see him as the 'last republican', offering a final opportunity of instituting a stable and ordered system of government before a descent into a chaos, to which, it must be said, Sulla had himself made a considerable contribution. He sought to put power where an *optimate* believed it should reside – with the senate and the nobility – and to ensure that sovereignty was vested in the men of influence in the *comitia centuriata*. He was trying to hedge such a system around with a protective fence of legislation, not fully appreciating perhaps that the strength of the traditional forms which he was trying to recreate lay precisely in the fact that they had been accepted and had not needed the protection of legislation. As Sulla himself had more than adequately demonstrated, and as Cicero was to observe in a later context, laws have little effect when faced with armed force.

Sulla thus set out to remove or neutralise by his laws all those elements in the Roman political machinery which over the previous half-century had, in his view, worked to undermine the primacy of the senate. However, as was (and still is) so often the case, the political leader was basing his programme on an attempt to deal with symptoms rather than to identify and treat causes.

The senate itself required attention; new members were added both to increase its numbers and to ensure its political sympathy with Sulla. Most notable was the recruitment of three hundred equestrians, who probably included both wealthy men from the business community in Rome and from 'worthy' Italian families. This made the senate representative of a slightly wider range of interests than before and made sure that there were sufficient senators available to supply the jurors who were to be needed in Sulla's reform of the legal system (see p.46). It is a matter of argument, and hardly capable now of certain resolution, whether his motive was to draw the senatorial and equestrian orders closer together or to neutralise the equestrian order by removing its leading members. Sulla also made the senate for the first time in its history an elected body, albeit indirectly; for he abolished the censorship, and laid down that for the future the senate's membership would be annually enhanced by the previous year's quaestors, whose number he raised to twenty.

The previous half-century had clearly shown up the chief threats to which the senate's primacy was vulnerable – magistrates, tribunes and provincial governors. All areas were tackled. In the case of the magistrates, the main danger emanated from those who managed to secure the protection and opportunity of office over an extended period, either by 'hogging' a particular office or by passing from one office to another with little or no interval. The examples of men like Marius and Cinna were clearly in Sulla's mind. Thus, he reinforced the old *lex annalis*, which had sought to regulate the *cursus honorum*; minimum ages were laid down for each office, so that there would be clear intervals between offices and nobody could reach the consulship before his early 40s, when the first flush of youthful ambition might be thought to have passed. In addition, Sulla enforced an interval of ten years between tenures of the same office, and a regulation that nobody could hold more than one office at the same time – a regulation which he himself breached in 80 BC. As we have seen, he raised the number of quaestors to twenty; he also increased the number of praetors to eight, so that each year there would be sufficient ex-consuls and ex-praetors to fill the vacancies for provincial governors. The free hand that some magistrates had demonstrated was checked by the rule which Sulla had first introduced in 88 BC ensuring that magistrates discussed legislative proposals in the senate before taking them to the *comitia*.

With the tribunate, Sulla was ruthless; he would, after all, have remembered the treatment that he himself had received at the hand of Sulpicius Rufus, as well as the numerous occasions on which tribunes had bypassed the senate and dealt directly with the plebeian assembly. It is not clear whether Sulla actually went as far as abolishing the sovereignty of the plebeian assembly or whether he simply required tribunes to seek senatorial approval before they approached the assembly. In a sense, the question is academic because of his other moves against tribunes – limiting the application of the veto, and enacting that those who had held the tribunate were thereby ineligible for any further office. Thus, the tribunate became a 'dead end'; no man of ambition would ever seek to hold it.

Finally, provincial governorships received Sulla's attention, and here he was in effect trying to prevent the kind of situation of which he himself had been able to take advantage. We have seen that Sulla's system produced sufficient consuls and praetors each year to provide promagistrates for the provinces in the following year. This was meant both to provide for a regular annual turnover in the provinces and to ensure that, broadly, consuls and praetors constituted a civilian administration and that the command of armies was restricted to promagistrates. Although, under the terms of the *lex Sempronia* of Gaius Gracchus, the allocation of provinces to individuals was decided by lot before relevant magistrates were elected, Sulla gave the senate a measure of protective control by allowing it to decide which would be proconsular and which propraetorian provinces. Detailed regulations concerning the conduct of promagistrates were also introduced, and brought within the competence of a treason court (*quaestio de maiestate*). These regulations included provisions that promagistrates should not start wars without reference to the senate and people, should not leave their provinces during their year of office, but should depart within thirty days of the expiry of their terms of office. In this way, Sulla hoped to ensure that promagistrates would not again be able to use their armies as a means of exerting pressure on the government in Rome.

The most lasting element of Sulla's work, however, was his reform of the judicial system; here he intended to remove the administration of justice from the popular assemblies. Building on the system of permanent courts (*quaestiones perpetuae*), such as that already established for extortion, Sulla added courts to handle cases of murder, poisoning, forgery, treason, bribery, peculation and assault. The juries for these courts were to be provided exclusively from members of the senate, and their president would be a praetor.

No sooner was the edifice in place than in 79 BC Sulla resigned, and took no further interest in politics, dying the following year. The reasons behind his resignation baffled contemporaries and remain obscure. Julius Caesar is quoted as saying that Sulla's resignation was a sign of his political illiteracy, whilst the satirist Juvenal informs us that nearly two centuries later students were still being required to produce 'essays' on the subject of Sulla's retirement. He may have thought that his task was successfully completed, or that he had done all that he could, and the working of the system was up to others. Alternatively, in view of the fact that he died in 78 BC he may already have been feeling the effects of what had been a very stressful decade in politics.

The 70s BC, culminating in the joint consulship of Pompey and Crassus in 70 BC, saw the weaknesses and undoing of a great deal of Sulla's work. In any case, it is clear that few people looked at Sulla's work from the point of view of the opportunity which it afforded the senate to re-establish its hegemony; more saw it as curtailing their and their factions' 'rightful' hereditary ambitions. In any case, the abrasiveness with which Sulla's work had been carried through inevitably left many eager for vengeance.

The first move after Sulla's retirement demonstrated the real weakness of what the *dictator* had created. Marcus Aemilius Lepidus, once a bitter enemy of the Marian cause, was elected consul for 78 BC with no discouragement from Sulla and with the support of Pompey; his 'programme' was the partial undoing of the Sullan constitution, including the restoration of the tribunate. Whatever Lepidus' true motives, he fell out with his fellow consul (Quintus Lutatius Catulus) and, with his deputy (*legatus*), Marcus Junius Brutus, started raising troops in Italy. Early in 77 BC, Lepidus marched this army against Rome; the senate passed the *senatus consultum ultimum*, empowering the consuls to deal with the rebellion, and gave Pompey, who had raised troops privately, but who had so far enjoyed no senatorial office, a special grant of propraetorian *imperium*. Thus, Pompey turned on the man he had so recently supported; indeed, he was responsible for the execution of Brutus.

Pompey was thus launched on the career of illegality, violence and duplicity that was to make this one-time supporter of Sulla an object of hatred to the *optimates*. It was soon apparent how serious an error the senate had made in encouraging Pompey, for when, following his defeat of Brutus, he was ordered by the *proconsul*, Catulus, to disband his army, Pompey's response was that he should be sent with a special proconsular *imperium* to aid Metellus Pius in Spain in the pursuit and eradication of the remnants of Marius' supporters, who were led by the talented Quintus Sertorius. The senate conceded, and Pompey, despite still not being a senator, enjoyed the standing of an ex-consul on a level with Metellus Pius. This was precisely the kind of irregularity that Sulla had sought to prevent, and the fact that Pompey restored peace in Spain could not alter the political damage that his appointment had done.

With one exception, the problems of the 70s BC remained in the foreign and military fields; the exception, however, was important. As we have seen, Sulla's legislation had borne down particularly toughly on the office of tribune of the plebs; as early as 79 BC, Lepidus had opened the debate on the future of the office, and by the mid-70s BC there was a considerable campaign underway, although, not surprisingly, its leading lights were the younger members of the nobility. One of these was Julius Caesar who, as a patrician, was personally ineligible for the office, but who was taking every opportunity at this stage to identify himself as the enemy of the authoritarianism and corruption which characterised the Sullan age. The campaign won a few concessions, such as the removal of the bar on further office, but full restoration of the tribunes' powers and privileges had to await the joint consulship of Pompey and Crassus in 70 BC.

Caesar was also involved in unsuccessful attempts to prosecute notoriously corrupt provincial governors. These cases highlighted the venality of courts dominated by senators; but one such case was successful – that brought in 70 BC against Gaius Verres by the people of Sicily, who secured the services of Cicero as prosecutor. This was Cicero's first major oration as a prosecutor, and it considerably enhanced his reputation. The case also contributed to the growing awareness of the vicious corruption that surrounded many of Sulla's supporters, and did little to enhance the reputation of the *optimates* or of senatorial government.

In three further military episodes, the rules laid down by Sulla were breached. In 74 BC a special command was given to Marcus Antonius (the father of Caesar's associate) to bring the pirates of the Mediterranean under control. Antonius proved ineffectual, and the problem of piracy remained as serious as ever and provided the excuse in 67 BC for giving an extensive command to Pompey.

In the same year (74 BC), it became clear that new action would be required to keep Mithridates under control. In the previous year, Rome's 'friend and ally' Nicomedes of Bithynia, had willed his kingdom to Rome, and the senate's acceptance of the bequest was the signal for Mithridates himself to aim a pre-emptive strike at Bithynia. Contrary to Sulla's rules, the incumbent consuls of 74 BC, Marcus Aurelius Cotta and Lucius Licinius Lucullus, were sent into the area – Cotta in charge of Bithynia and Lucullus in charge of the provinces of Asia and Cilicia, as well as of the actual war against Mithridates.

The last of these military problems – the revolt of the Thracian gladiator Spartacus in 73 BC – proved to be the catalyst to the final dissolution of Sulla's constitutional arrangements. Spartacus caused considerable disruption in Italy and defeated the consuls of 72 BC who had been sent against him. The republic's armies were thus left under the command of Marcus Crassus, one of the praetors of the year. He fared better, defeating and killing Spartacus, though not before, in something of a panic, the senate and people had voted that Crassus should share his command with Pompey, freshly returned from Spain. Pompey, to Crassus' annoyance, claimed half of the glory, even though his contribution had been little more than to mop up a few stragglers after Spartacus' defeat.

The *optimates* in the senate may have hoped that their own political salvation would be secured by Pompey and Crassus turning their armies against each other. No love had ever been lost between these two supporters of Sulla, and Crassus, along with others, would have viewed Pompey's illegal rise during the 70s BC with envy and disquiet. The anxieties were more than confirmed by Pompey's arrogance in the war against Spartacus. However, the denouement was not to be; instead, these two rivals decided to form a temporary political partnership (*amicitia*), pooling their wealth, their armies and their clientage in a bid for the consulship of 70 BC on a programme that involved the removal of what was left of Sulla's constitution. With their armies as a powerful coercive force, Crassus and Pompey found little difficulty in securing the senate's acquiescence to their demands; in addition, Pompey was granted a triumph for his Spanish victory, and Crassus an ovation – a lesser form of the triumph – for his success against Spartacus. Crassus was, under Sulla's *lex annalis*, qualified to hold the

49

consulship, whilst Pompey was too young and had held none of the qualifying offices; Pompey, in fact, was still not even a member of the senate.

Thus, the stage was set not just for the dismantling of Sulla's constitution: the rivalry between Pompey and Crassus initiated a chain of events that demonstrated decisively the inability of senate and people to govern Rome and the empire.

6

The domination of Pompey

The joint consulship of Pompey and Crassus in 70 BC may have undone the main features of Sulla's constitution, but it had not diminished the thirst for power on the part of *optimates*. The senate as an organ of government was, of course, immeasurably weakened not just by the events of 70 BC, but also by its inability during the 70s BC to take up the opportunity that Sulla had tried to give it; by 70 BC, all the threats to its supremacy that Sulla had set out to neutralise were once again evident.

It is often said that, after their consulship, Pompey and Crassus retired, as if they had no further interest in power. This would have been uncharacteristic of them; but the view is in any case quite inconsistent with the evidence. It is true that most of the magistrates of the years 69–67 BC were from the *optimate* factions, and that the most important military command of the period – that against Mithridates – was in the hands of the Sullan Lucullus; but the fact that two of the tribunes of 67 BC, Gaius Cornelius and Aulus Gabinius, undertook, amongst other things, a substantial legislative programme aimed at corruption in government (including electoral corruption) shows that *optimate* dominance in those years must have been achieved against strong opposition. Further, the great commands – against the pirates and against Mithridates – which Pompey was given in 67 and 66 BC did not come out of the blue, but represented the culmination of campaigns that

51

cannot have been conducted without the active encouragement of Pompey and Crassus.

For the moment at least there was a degree of accord between these two, even if their ultimate ambitions had them on a collision course. They had obviously declined to take proconsular provinces, partly perhaps because the most suitable venues were already taken up, but more to prepare the ground for future developments. It is obvious that the great networks of patronage and political intrigue that surround Pompey and Crassus in the middle and later 60s BC were not built up overnight.

Although both had come to notice as part of Sulla's *optimate* faction, it is not surprising that neither of them retained any credit with *optimates* in the early 60s BC. Both had turned in new directions: Crassus had established himself as the patron of equestrian businessmen, whilst Pompey looked partly in that direction also, although his triumphalism led him to court the enthusiasm of the urban plebs. Current problems in foreign and domestic politics, therefore, had a relevance to both Pompey and Crassus.

Piracy in the Mediterranean was a long-standing problem. Pirates were in many cases refugees from political intolerance in their own states and secured themselves in rocky and inaccessible bases, particularly on Crete and along the southern coast of Asia Minor (the Roman province of Cilicia). During the heyday of the great Greek navies, the pirates had been adequately checked, but Rome's elimination of Greek naval power and her failure to introduce an alternative left a vacuum in which piracy flourished. The pirates disrupted trade, thus threatening vital supplies to Italy, and were even landing on the Italian coast, kidnapping and pillaging.

Rome's steps to check the Mediterranean pirates had been woefully inadequate: Marcus Antonius had been sent east in 102 BC, and his son (of the same name) had been given a special command in 74 BC, which had achieved nothing; indeed the problem had worsened as a result of Rome's preoccupation with Mithridates and because the pirates gained strength from his success. The most recent attempt to stamp out the pirates had been made in 68–67 BC by Quintus Metellus (Creticus), who had formally added Crete to the empire. It was in everyone's interest, but particularly that of the businessmen and ordinary citizens, that this problem be eradicated, and clearly such a job would bring enormous opportunities to the man who successfully completed it.

The conduct of the third Mithridatic War, which broke out in 74 BC, had been committed to the *optimate* Lucullus as governor of Asia. In military terms, the early years of Lucullus' command were successful, and by 70 BC Mithridates was nearly a 'spent force'. Two factors, however, complicated the issue. First, the equilibrium of Asia Minor was delicate at the best of times because of the ambitions not just of Mithridates but also of other regional rulers. A particularly difficult character was Mithridates' son-in-law, Tigranes of Armenia, who gave refuge to his father-in-law after his defeat by Lucullus. Lucullus, who had asked a lot of his troops in four years' campaigning, pushed them beyond the limit of their endurance by embarking in appalling conditions on a campaign to capture Armenia. His effectiveness as a commander did not survive this enterprise. Second, Lucullus had done something to try to alleviate the financial disaster that had overtaken the provincials of Asia as a result of Sulla's harsh settlement of the area. However, alleviating the lot of provincials meant reducing the profits of Roman businessmen in the area; and although Lucullus was remembered as something of a hero in Asia, with a festival named after him, equestrians were determined to be rid of him.

That a campaign against Lucullus was organised in Rome is in no doubt; that Crassus and Pompey were involved in it seems very likely, particularly in view of the fact that Lucullus' brother-in-law, Publius Claudius Pulcher (who preferred to be called Clodius, the plebeian form of his name), who was in Lucullus' entourage, set out to create disaffection in Lucullus' demoralised army. There is little doubt that, until 62 BC, Clodius was part of Pompey's mushrooming network of political supporters. Through 69 and 68 BC Lucullus' command was reduced by the gradual removal of his provinces, and in 67 BC, on a proposal of the Pompeian tribune Aulus Gabinius, the province of Bithynia/Pontus was reassigned.

But Gabinius' main bill (the *lex Gabinia* of 67 BC) was to create a special command with authority throughout the Mediterranean and vast resources, and to award it to an ex-consul. Clearly Pompey was meant, and, although some *optimates* tried opposition to or modification of the bill, their spokesmen amongst the tribunes were treated by Gabinius as Tiberius Gracchus had treated Octavius in 133 BC. Violence and corruption were rife on both sides, but Pompey got his command. From his point of view, apart from the fact that he relished this type of military and organisational challenge, the most attractive feature of the command would have been the large-scale patronage that was his to dispense; not least, Gabinius' bill had allowed Pompey the appointment of twenty-four deputies (*legati*). Men could thus be put under obligation to Pompey, and the names which we know read like a roll-call of Pompey's faction. As was the case for Marius forty years earlier, however, success for Pompey was essential: in fact, within three months the problem of piracy was solved, and, as before in Spain, Pompey set about a thoughtful programme of post-war settlement which was designed to ensure stability.

Pompey was now at the crest of his reputation; his success ensured widespread popularity and demonstrated to businessmen and politicians of all ages that the route to success for them lay through Pompey. As he himself observed, no Roman had ever commanded a larger or broader field of patronage. On the other hand, a career such as his, laced as it was with illegality, violence and political treachery, ensured that he had made enemies.

Pompey's success against the pirates made it inevitable that he would now be given the command against Mithridates: so, one of the tribunes of 66 BC, Gaius Manilius, with vocal support from the young Julius Caesar and from Marcus Cicero (praetor in 66 BC), proposed that the Mithridatic war should now be entrusted to Pompey, and that he should retain the forces and resources which he had recently used to such good effect against the pirates. There was opposition, but it had little chance of defeating Manilius; Cicero's speech on the occasion, which survives (*Pro lege Manilia*), no doubt articulated a general feeling that Pompey, who was almost a monarch in the east, was the only guarantor of prosperity and stability.

Predictably, Lucullus did not agree, complaining bitterly about Pompey as 'the carrion-bird who feasted on others' leftovers'. There was some justice in Lucullus' complaint; he had blunted Mithridates at the height of his power, and the Mithridates whom Pompey faced and who committed suicide in 63 BC, after nearly sixty years on his throne, was a shadow of his former self. Although a wise settlement of the east, depending upon a network of provinces and client-kingdoms in Asia Minor, deservedly brought Pompey more credit, one feature of his campaigns – the involving of the king of Parthia in Rome's eastern arrangements – was to create a 'running sore' that was still as troublesome as ever in the third century AD.

Pompey's patronage produced for him a network of supporters in Rome, though controlling them from a distance was not so easy. Further, there were enemies, such as the *optimates* smarting over the fate of Lucullus, and rivals, such as Crassus, who were waiting for the opportunity to erode Pompey's standing (*auctoritas*). Crassus, who was never a man to act openly, preferred to manipulate; in particular, he wanted to construct a position for himself whereby Pompey would have to take him seriously as a political force; nor was he averse to undermining Pompey's support where he could and winning disaffected Pompeians into his own patronage. As censor in 65 BC Crassus first tried to give full citizenship to the Italians beyond the river Po (Cisalpine Gaul); it was an area where Pompey had some influence because of his father's patronage interests, and which might prove valuable for its manpower. Crassus failed, as he probably anticipated, but was remembered well for his attempt. Second he also organised a special command for Gnaeus Calpurnius Piso in Spain, an area with good memories of Pompey from the 70s BC. It is not clear what precisely was at stake, though the historian Sallust leaves the broad issue in no doubt when he informs us that Piso was murdered by friends of Pompey. Third, Crassus tried to have Egypt organised as a Roman province under the terms of the probably spurious will of its late king, Ptolemy X. The attraction of Egypt to Crassus was possibly its proximity to Pompey's theatre of operations, but more likely its wealth, which would enhance his patronage, and its commercial opportunities, which would develop his ties with the equestrians. Crassus was opposed by the *optimates*, who did not relish his dominance any more than they did Pompey's, and by Cicero who, in a partly preserved speech (*De rege Alexandrino*), argued that the whole matter was an attempt to weaken Pompey. Thus, Crassus' initiatives came to nothing.

Inevitably, the greater threat to Pompey was from within his own network of supporters. These, as was usual in Roman politics, were not held together by commonly-held beliefs and policies but by a recognition that Pompey's support offered them their best opportunities for advancement. Without doubt, many of Pompey's supporters were eager for glory – and were unscrupulous. In the mid-60s BC in Rome, it was probably Cicero and his arch-rival, Catiline (Lucius Sergius Catilina), who were most disruptive of the stability of Pompey's faction. A sequence of events started in 66 BC that was by the late 60s BC to bring Pompey to an embarrassed ineffectiveness.

The consuls elected for 65 BC, Publius Autronius Paetus and Publius Cornelius Sulla (the *dictator's* nephew), were disqualified for electoral corruption; neither was a friend of Pompey. Either at the time of the original election or at the time of the rerun, Catiline, who wished to be a candidate, was disqualified because he had a charge hanging over him of malpractice during his propraetorship in Africa in 67 BC. In the rerun election the successful candidates were Lucius Aurelius Cotta and Lucius Manlius Torquatus, the latter of whom was associated with Pompey. The story was subsequently related by Cicero in his own election address in 64 BC (*oratio in toga candida*), when he and Catiline were rivals for the consulship of 63 BC, that on 1 January 65 BC, Catiline had been part of a conspiracy to murder the incoming consuls with the objective either of himself sharing the vacancies with Autronius or of restoring Autronius and Sulla. Some accounts alleged the involvement also of Crassus and Caesar, though it has to be said that such a bizarre move ill accords with Crassus' normal approach. Nothing happened because Catiline (or, in some accounts, Caesar) failed to give a correct signal.

It is clear that at the time the facts relating to this so-called 'first conspiracy of Catiline' were very thin and thus ready for the kind of embellishment that Cicero, when it later suited him, was so well qualified to provide; 'who is there', Cicero was later to allege, 'who does not know that on the first of January you were poised with your dagger to kill the consuls in the forum?'. A few facts survive, which provide a vivid demonstration of the corruption of Roman politics and serve to demonstrate the improbability of Cicero's later assertion. A letter of Cicero's, written in 65 BC to his friend Atticus, contains the statement that he was hoping to defend Catiline in his trial for governmental malpractice, and that the prosecutor (Publius Clodius) was prepared to collude with the defence. Catiline evidently declined the offer, for we find in a later Ciceronian speech the information that Catiline was in fact defended by Lucius Manilius Torquatus, the consul whom he was allegedly about to murder. Would Cicero seriously have contemplated defending Catiline if the latter had been involved in such a plot?

The link between most of the protagonists was the patronage of Pompey, and a fragmentary inscription survives establishing a link between Pompey's family and that of Catiline. The events make more sense if viewed as an attempt by Pompeians first to discredit the men originally elected to the consulship and then to defend their own replacements with force if necessary against an *optimate* plot to unseat them. Thus, Catiline's role was not to murder Torquatus, as Cicero later unashamedly asserted, but to defend him. It was possibly at this point that Crassus saw an opportunity to offer support to some of those involved in these events – Catiline, Clodius and, perhaps, Caesar too.

The cabal was none too edifying and may not have done Pompey a great deal of good. But worse was to come; in 64 BC Cicero and Catiline came forward as rival candidates for the consulship – a rivalry which plainly Cicero had hoped to avoid by his offer to defend Catiline the previous year. Cicero, facing the uphill task of winning election to the consulship as a 'new man', needed the support of Pompey's partisans. So, if Catiline would not co-operate, Cicero saw no alternative but to subject him to a public demolition (the *oratio in toga candida*). His search for widespread support will not have endeared him to Pompey, for he sought the favour of the *optimates* not only by defending Pompey's enemy, Gaius Piso, the consul of 67 BC, and blocking an attempt, which Pompey and Caesar favoured, to rehabilitate the sons of the victims of Sulla's proscriptions, but also by promising Lucullus help in his quest for a well-deserved triumph which predictably Pompey opposed.

Cicero was elected, along with Gaius Antonius (uncle of Caesar's later associate, Marcus Antonius); Catiline, despite disappointment and incorrect assertions that he now turned to conspiracy, lived to fight another day. Immediately, Cicero was pitched into a new controversy; one of the new tribunes of 63 BC, Publius Servilius Rullus, about whom we know very little, proposed a *lex agraria*. This was vigorously opposed by Cicero in a group of speeches which survive (*orationes de lege agraria*) on the ground that it was an attempt on Crassus' part to create difficulties for Pompey in his settlement of the east by sending (as was normal) a commission of ten to assist. Cicero strangely seems to imply that the activation of due process was an insult to Pompey, organised by Rullus 'and those whom one fears more than one does Rullus'. It seems likely that Cicero made a complete error here: the bill, which appears to have dealt with the eastern settlement, with the provision of land which Pompey would soon need for the discharge of his veterans, and with the vexed problems of debt and the status of the sons of the proscribed, may well have been the brainchild of Pompey rather than of Crassus. In successfully opposing it in Pompey's name, Cicero not only created obvious difficulties for Pompey but also alienated from the general some of the support that he was trying to win by it. This would provide a far more cogent explanation of Pompey's coolness towards Cicero, which both hurt and mystified him, than other more flimsy reasons that have been proposed.

The dominating event of 63 BC was, of course, the Catilinarian conspiracy, in which Catiline appears to have made a serious attempt to assassinate Cicero and to embroil the republic in revolution. At this distance, it is very hard to assess the gravity of the threat posed by Catiline; though there is no doubt that Cicero regarded it seriously, it is evident that he experienced considerable difficulty in convincing his fellow senators of it.

The drama began when Catiline stood for the consulship of 62 BC. From the outset, Cicero concentrated attention on the havoc that Catiline would wreak as consul and the threat of disruption to the election itself. Cicero asked the senate to vote him a bodyguard and, when it refused, formed one privately. One of those who rallied to his support was Publius Clodius. In a display calculated to alarm, Cicero appeared at the election wearing his breastplate under his toga. Catiline lost again, and this appears to have precipitated him into more desperate measures. The chief plank of Catiline's platform was the cancellation of debts, which, according to Cicero later, had never been more burdensome. The proposal appealed widely – to ordinary debtors, to aristocrats who had squandered their resources and, in particular, to Sullan veterans who had been settled on land but who had not made a success of farming. These were to provide the backbone of the army with which Catiline was later to threaten the city. Cicero had no sympathy for such a proposal and saw its rejection as essential to the maintenance of sound financial order and to preserving the goodwill of the equestrian order.

Although Cicero was kept well informed of Catiline's plans for an uprising on 28 October, it was not until 21 October that he was able to persuade the senate grudgingly to pass the *senatus consultum ultimum*. Following the failure of an assassination attempt on Cicero, Catiline left Rome early in November to take personal charge of his army in the field; revised plans were made for an insurrection in Rome on 17 December. Cicero's lack of documented evidence was eventually resolved by a Gallic deputation whose members had been approached by Catiline's friends in Rome, and on 4 December the consul was able to arrest the conspirators; on the following day, the question of their fate was put before the senate.

Herein lay an important problem; strictly, the senate had no competence except to decide the charges upon which the conspirators should be tried – in this case, murder or riot. Cicero, however, took the view that as the *senatus consultum ultimum* had been passed, the senate could effectively condemn them. Legally, this was not correct, and ironically, earlier in the year, Caesar had brought a rather bizarre case against one Rabirius for his participation in the actions which followed the passing of the *senatus consultum ultimum* in 100 BC. The trial was stopped by Cicero, but Caesar had made his point. In the debate on the fate of the conspirators as recorded by Sallust, several senators, including the young Marcus Cato, 'our hero', as Cicero was later to call him, argued for the implementation of the death penalty. Caesar proposed an alternative punishment of life imprisonment (which did not exist in the penal code) and argued strongly that the *senatus consultum ultimum* could not override a citizen's right of appeal.

Cicero won the day, and the conspirators in Rome were executed; Catiline himself was killed at the head of his army early in the following year. A grateful populace hailed Cicero as 'father of the country', and the consul basked in a glory which he later endeavoured to keep alive by writing accounts of his consulship. However, his execution of the conspirators, necessary as he may have thought it, was to cause him much trouble; he had acted illegally, and he had done it in the interests of Pompey. Again, he could hardly have expected the general's gratitude; the point was made thoroughly clear to him when, almost without precedent, his valedictory address as consul was vetoed by one of the new tribunes – Metellus Nepos, recently returned from acting as one of Pompey's *legati* in the east. Eventually, Cicero was to pay a higher price for his illegality.

Much more broadly, the events of 63 BC seemed to Cicero to demonstrate a political philosophy in action – what is commonly referred to as the 'union of the orders' (*concordia ordinum*). Cicero's own beliefs owed less to factional imperatives than was the case with the majority of his contemporaries, and these beliefs had much in common with those enunciated by Polybius a century previously. For Cicero, the stability of Rome depended upon the rule of law; law was respected because it was the expression of reason. In political terms, reason was represented by the paternalism of an enlightened oligarchy – the 'good men', or *boni*, as Cicero called them. Essentially, the *boni* were the *optimates*, though without their more bigoted adherents for whom Cicero had little time, and joined by equestrians and Italians who shared a patriotic love of Rome. This union of senators, equestrians and Italians was Cicero's *concordia ordinum*, and all looked to the senate for governmental leadership. The security and stability of the *concordia* was to be guaranteed by a senior individual, a man of exceptional standing (*auctoritas*) enjoying respect for his wealth, achievements and patronage but not holding any particular office; in Roman terms, such a leading citizen was a *princeps*. Cicero referred to this person as the *rector* or *moderator*; sometimes Cicero thought historically and seems to have had Scipio Aemilianus in mind, but when he applied his thinking to contemporary politics, the figure in his mind was Pompey.

For Cicero, the elimination of the threat posed by Catiline would facilitate the restoration of the proper functioning of the republic. Indeed, his judgement was at fault not only in this misinterpretation, but also in his view of *how* the republic survived the assault of Catiline's conspiracy. Throughout his life Cicero continued to believe that Catiline had been blocked by an impressive coalition of senators, equestrians and Italians whose first thought was the good of the republic; for him, therefore, the episode represented positive proof of the efficacy of the *concordia ordinum*, and he was convinced that it would outlast these events and continue to guarantee the stability of the republic. Cicero ignored the difficulty that he had experienced in convincing the senatorial nobility of the criminality of Catiline, and also the fact that the closing of ranks behind him in 63 BC had been tardy, grudging and temporary.

The priorities of public figures were not as Cicero envisaged them: ambition was the constant victor over patriotism. The events of the three years that separated the Catilinarian conspiracy from the formation of the first triumvirate left Cicero increasingly despondent as he saw his coalition breaking apart under the strain. Two problems in particular, and the consequences of them, dominated the period: the desecration of the ceremony of the *Bona Dea* by Publius Clodius, and Pompey's return from the east.

It remains far from clear whether Clodius' gatecrashing, disguised as a woman, of the ceremonies held by the Vestal Virgins in honour of the *Bona Dea* should be seen as relevant to his public or his private life. This is partly because Clodius' previous career is known to us only through isolated incidents – his undermining of Lucullus' army in 68 BC, the collusive prosecution of Catiline in 65 BC and his membership of Cicero's private bodyguard in 63 BC. However, obscurity surrounds the incident also because the repercussions rapidly became more momentous than the incident itself. The ceremony was held at the house of Julius Caesar, who was chief priest (*pontifex maximus*) and urban praetor at the time; it has been suggested that Clodius' behaviour may have been aimed at embarrassing Caesar and that Clodius was pursuing a liaison with Caesar's wife. Alternatively, the idea may simply have appealed to him. It is certain that the incident made Clodius' a household name, and the seeking of publicity may have been a motive.

Marcus Cato, one of the tribunes of 62 BC, who had made a reputation for himself in the debate on the fate of the Catilinarian conspirators for his stern defence of tradition and old-fashioned morality, saw this as an even bigger challenge. The senate decided that a sacrilege had been committed and that Clodius should be tried; tampering with the jury was always likely to be an issue, and in the event Clodius was acquitted due to bribery on an extensive scale, organised, according to Cicero, by Marcus Crassus. Cicero's view of the jury was that 'you would not find a worse crew in a gambling-joint'. Later, Cicero took the view that the wiser course of action would have been to leave Clodius with the threat of action hanging over him.

For Clodius, an important feature of the trial was the failure of Cicero and Pompey, who he believed were in his debt, to help him; Cicero destroyed Clodius' alibi at his trial, whilst Pompey, who had to be very careful whom he offended at this stage, remained firmly aloof. Both were to pay a price for their 'disloyalty'. For Cato, who had taken the moral high ground, the discomfiture of Cicero was of little concern, whilst that of Pompey was positively welcome; *optimates*, smarting under Pompey's treatment of the Sullan constitution and, more recently, his humiliation of Lucullus, had little sympathy for the general.

More damaging was the moral fervour of Cato's anger towards the equestrian order following the corrupt acquittal of Clodius. Since the reform of the juries of the *quaestiones* carried out by Pompey and Crassus in 70 BC, equestrian jurors had exercised the dominant role. It could hardly have been expected that the *optimates* would fail to profit from what had happened. Apart from decrying the corruption, they were given the chance to demonstrate their displeasure when, in 61 BC, a group of equestrians who had won the contract to collect taxes in the province of Asia and who had found that, due to the ravages of war in the area, their profit margins could not be maintained, applied to the senate for a revision of their contract.

On this occasion, the equestrians were championed by their long-standing patron, Marcus Crassus. Cicero also supported them, for, although he thought their request to be completely out of line, he felt he had to maintain his influence with the equestrians and do whatever he could to prevent an open breach between senators and equestrians. His efforts, however, were in vain, for the senate, strongly influenced by Cato, took the view that it was not its responsibility to rescue equestrians who had simply been too greedy in the first place. Cicero, accusing Cato of behaving as if he lived in 'Plato's Republic', knew that this was a mortal blow to his dreams of a *concordia*; Crassus' problem was more pressing, in that he would lose face with his clients if he failed to secure what they required of him.

In this respect, therefore, the consequences of the 'Clodius affair' were extremely damaging; but worse was to follow. At the end of 62 BC, Pompey arrived back in Italy after five years of successful campaigning; many will have feared that he would repeat Sulla's course of action and take Rome by force. The fact that he did not has caused commentators and historians considerable difficulty. Pompey, it is argued, was a constitutionalist at heart to whom such a course of action would have been repugnant; but Pompey had rarely put the interests of the constitution above his own. More likely, Pompey's action in disbanding his troops was born of his characteristic arrogance; on this occasion, he probably thought that he had the popularity and influence to be able to carry the day in whatever he wanted.

He was, however, mistaken; the *optimates*, sensing that without his army Pompey would be more amenable, refused to co-operate with him. Cato, who was after all only a tribune in 62 BC, refused the offer of a marriage alliance between his family and Pompey's, which would normally have been regarded as of great advantage to the 'junior' man. Pompey, however, needed the senate's goodwill, since his eastern settlement required ratification by the senate and people, and his discharged soldiers required the passage of a *lex agraria* to provide land for their settlement.

When Pompey returned, the 'burning issue' was Clodius' sacrilege; in view of all that was involved, Pompey attempted to sit on the fence, making a speech which, according to Cicero, pleased nobody but consisted mainly of rather empty references to his steadfast respect for the senate. Such views will have made little impression on senators or on Clodius, who obviously expected more of his patron. Further, Pompey greatly annoyed Cicero by his coolness to him, which stemmed partly from Cicero's demolition in 63 BC of the Rullan legislation, and partly from the fact that the orator, with his invitations to Pompey to join with him for the good of the republic, appeared to Pompeian eyes to be taking too much for granted.

Pompey's failure to achieve his requirements through the senate and people led him in 60 BC to try to achieve his ends through Lucius Flavius, one of the tribunes, who seems to have undertaken what amounted to a resuscitation of the Rullan legislation. This met opposition not only from Pompey's enemies but also from people, like Cicero, who disliked what they regarded as injurious to financial stability. Cicero, indeed, could be relied upon to oppose what he regarded as detrimental to the economic interests of the equestrian order; debt alleviation was in his eyes as dangerous when sponsored by Pompey as it had been when it had formed part of Catiline's programme.

The political temperature ran very high, but Lucius Flavius achieved nothing, leaving Pompey as far away as ever from realising his ends. The year 60 BC also saw the return of Julius Caesar from a propraetorship in Spain; Caesar's immediate requirement was for the senate to approve a triumph for his achievements in Spain. He also wanted to stand as a candidate for the consulship of 59 BC. There was an element of inconsistency in these requests which the *optimates* hoped to exploit; for, to receive a triumph, the applying general had to await the senate's decision outside the city limits, whilst candidates for office had to make their nominations personally to the presiding officer.

The *optimates* clearly hoped to stall Caesar on both counts; in the event, Caesar gave up his triumph and presented himself as a candidate. It is unlikely that Caesar had failed to anticipate what would happen, and the episode probably illustrates a tactic which he not infrequently employed – that of putting his opponents morally in the wrong for being unreasonable enough to cross him.

Given the confidence of the *optimates*, Caesar's election to a consulship was by no means guaranteed; thus, the idea of a political *amicitia* appears to have been born – probably secretly at first. Caesar's candidature would be linked with that of Lucius Lucceius, a friend of Pompey's, whilst Pompey and Crassus would put their resources and clientage at the disposal of both in return for an undertaking that Pompey's and Crassus' frustrated requirements would be satisfactorily resolved during 59 BC. The enterprise was not totally successful; for whilst Caesar was elected, Lucceius was not, and Caesar was left with Marcus Calpurnius Bibulus as his colleague – an *optimate* and close friend of Cato, who had sanctioned bribery on a large scale to secure Bibulus' election.

Thus, the compact known to history as the first triumvirate had come into being, and it was clearly the intention of the three men to exercise dominance over the governmental machinery, partly through Caesar's tenure of the consulship and partly through their combined political influence.

The 60s BC had been Pompey's heyday; throughout the decade, his figure had dominated Roman politics and much that was done was prompted by a desire either to please him or to oppose him. At the end of the decade, that influence was perhaps a little beyond its peak, for Pompey had been shown through 61 and 60 BC to be vulnerable to opposition. None the less, the mass of his wealth and the breadth of his clientage meant not only that he was the driving force behind the triumvirate but that he remained the most powerful man in Rome; further, his continuing cynical attitude to alliances and friendships made him amongst the most unpredictable and dangerous of Roman politicians. It was not for nothing that, early on, he had earned the sobriquet of *adulescentulus carnifex*, 'youthful executioner'; nothing was allowed to stand in the way of the ambitions of Pompeius Magnus.

7

The first triumvirate and the slide to civil war

Unlike the second triumvirate formed in 43 BC by Marcus Antonius (Marc Antony), Octavian and Lepidus, the first remained a private compact (*amicitia*), not an instrument of government. Although at first even the existence of the triumvirate was known probably to only a few, it soon became an object of criticism, even detestation. The satirist Varro called it the 'three-headed monster'; Cicero, who had been invited to join it, attacked it because, in his view, it diverted Pompey from his true destiny – as an ally of the senate and as *moderator* in a 'Ciceronian' republic. The Augustan historian Asinius Pollio blamed it for the outbreak of the civil war in 49 BC and thus, by implication, for the final collapse of the republic. Yet, as we have seen, its aims were relatively modest and reasonable, and it had been forced into existence more by the intransigence of the *optimates* than by outlandish ambitions on the part of the three themselves. Ultimately, however, the three can be seen, together with others, as rivals for the support of the *populares* amongst the nobility, the equestrians, and the urban and rural plebs.

The first months of Caesar's consulship (59 BC) were taken up with moves to secure the resolution of the issues which had brought the three together in the first place. The *optimates*, buoyant over their success at having Bibulus elected as Caesar's consular colleague, continued to be obstructive. Thus, after an initial attempt to propose a *lex agraria* through the normal

66

channels of senate and people had been blocked, Caesar exercised his constitutional prerogative and took his bill directly to the *comitia*. The principal aim of the bill was to acquire land for distribution to Pompey's veterans; other welfare measures that had featured in the failed bills of Rullus (63 BC) and Flavius (60 BC) were probably also included. To allay fears, Caesar promised that the land commission, which was to be set up under the bill to administer the acquisition and distribution of land, would deal only with land that came naturally on to the market and would not touch the good agricultural land of Campania, which was close enough to Rome to be viewed as a highly sensitive place of settlement for Pompey's veterans. It was probably the poor supply of land, rather than vindictiveness on Caesar's part, that by April had caused him to go back on this undertaking and bring in a fresh bill (*lex Campana*) which put Campanian land at the disposal of the land commissioners.

Other necessary legislation was pursued by the tribune Publius Vatinius in the plebeian assembly; Pompey's eastern arrangements were ratified, and one-third of the Asian tax contract bid was remitted to the equestrians. Vatinius also saw to Caesar's needs; for some time it had been evident that attention was going to have to be given to the stability of western Europe. As had happened in the late second century BC, population movements in central Europe were putting pressure on those who lived near them. In particular, Ariovistus, chief of the Suebi who lived on the eastern bank of the Rhine, was forced to cross the river in search of new homelands; this, in its turn, put pressure on to those tribes of central Gaul who were Rome's allies. Similarly, the tribe of the Helvetii (in modern Switzerland) wished to make a peaceful migration to new homes in southwest Gaul and hoped to be able to save time and effort by going through the Roman province of Gallia Transalpina.

The threat of war in Gaul was clear, although immediately it was averted by recognising Ariovistus as an ally of Rome. However, before the consular elections of 60 BC, the senate had named the 'woodlands and paths' of Italy as a proconsular province for the consuls of 59 BC – a sinecure either to leave the consuls to all intents and purposes free should it be necessary to send an emergency expedition to Gaul, or, as some thought, to ensure that Caesar did not receive an armed province.

Vatinius, in fact, passed a bill that gave Caesar Cisalpine Gaul and Illyricum with three legions for five years; this was an appointment which commenced immediately (probably on 1 March 59 BC) rather than, as would have been normal, after the expiry of Caesar's consulship. Later in the year, Gallia Transalpina was added as well, though apparently under the normal conditions of appointment, such as annual tenure.

It is little wonder that the popularity of the triumvirate was waning: not only was it becoming clear that the constitution was effectively dominated by Pompey's veterans and Caesar's Gallic army but also the three acquired considerable sums of money with which to finance support and thus increase popularity through a very suspect deal by which they recognised Ptolemy Auletes as the rightful king of Egypt.

Optimates were enthusiastic in their support of Bibulus who, sensing that he would not be able to stop Caesar by normal means, had elected 'to watch the sky for omens', a religious manoeuvre which properly should have brought Caesar's legislative programme to a halt; in succeeding years, it certainly left a significant question mark hanging over the legitimacy of what Caesar did in 59 BC. Even the plebs cooled in their enthusiasm, and Cicero began to sense the disintegration of the triumvirate which to him would have provided Pompey with the opportunity he needed to desert his colleagues and ally with Cicero and the senate.

Caesar, in particular, was intolerant of opposition, whilst Pompey was affected by a morbid fear of assassination and, in any case, hated to witness signs of his unpopularity. It was following a speech in the spring of 59 BC in which Cicero gave vent to his criticisms of the current situation that Caesar and Pompey participated in a move that was to have profound and unexpected results. For some time, Publius Clodius had been attempting to secure a renunciation of his patrician status in order to become a plebeian; this was an essential prerequisite to his competing for the office of tribune of the plebs. After a number of failed attempts to do this, Clodius' change of status was suddenly facilitated by Caesar (as *pontifex maximus*) and Pompey (as *augur*). There can be little doubt that they hoped to be able to use Clodius, as tribune in 58 BC, to cow the opposition in general of the *optimates* and in particular of men like Marcus Cato and Cicero. The hope of Caesar and Pompey was not unreasonable, since such a service as they had performed would normally have entailed political repayment.

But Clodius' ambitions left little space for the normal niceties of political conduct: he had aims of his own, and looked to Caesar and Pompey to help serve them. In the short term, Clodius wished to exact revenge on Pompey, Cicero and Cato, by all of whom he believed himself to have been betrayed and undermined at the time of the *Bona Dea* trial in 61 BC; in the longer term, he wished to repeat the exercise of the Gracchi and use the office of tribune as a power base to acquire the support of the urban plebs as a means of domination. His legislation in 58 BC indicated that he saw the tribune's office, however, as a way of acquiring the means to conduct a far more intimidatory brand of politics with street gangs. Clodius aspired to primacy amongst the *populares*, and in this respect the three were his rivals.

The three realised that they needed to support each other, and that the detachment of any one of them would pose a serious threat to the other two. With Caesar due to leave for his province at the beginning of January 58 BC, and neither Pompey nor Crassus in office, the services of others were essential. If Clodius were to prove a disappointment, then success in the consular elections for 58 BC for Lucius Piso (Caesar's father-in-law) and Aulus Gabinius (Pompey's long-term associate) seemed to guarantee a stable position for the three. It is possible that the allegation by an informer, named Vettius, that a number of *optimates* were plotting against Pompey's life, was an attempt masterminded by Caesar to ensure that any temptation that Pompey might feel to desert to the *optimates* would be short-lived. Alternatively, Clodius may have been behind the 'Vettius affair', seeing it as a way of denying Cicero and those *optimates* whom he wished to attack any possible support from Pompey, who remained the most influential figure in Roman politics. The questions of whether there really was a plot against Pompey's life, and whether, if there was, it involved all or any of those named almost pales into insignificance.

At the opening of his tribunician year, Clodius lost little time in putting forward to the plebeian assembly a group of measures which had the objectives of advancing his own dominance and protecting him from attack. The introduction of a free grain dole to all citizens won him much support, as well as proving so costly that it drained other projects, such as the work of Caesar's land commission, of funds; Clodius' legalisation of trades guilds proved to be the means by which he could recruit the street gangs that were to become a dominant feature of Roman politics for the rest of the 50s BC. At the same time, he restricted the powers of the censors to remove senators and outlawed the kind of religious manoeuvring that Bibulus had employed against Caesar.

The intimidatory power of the gangs was immediately seen as Clodius proceeded against Cicero; outlawing those who had denied to Roman citizens their right to appeal to the people – of which, of course, Cicero was guilty in his handling of the Catilinarian affair – was a neat way of encompassing the ruin of a man whom he viewed as a possible rival and on whom, in any case, he wished to have his revenge. The penalty exacted from Cicero might also serve to deter anyone in 58 BC from trying to use the *senatus consultum ultimum* against Clodius himself. Cicero was exiled, and, in a move that was to cause the orator difficulty later, Clodius had Cicero's house demolished and the site consecrated as a shrine to *libertas*.

Although the moves to have Cicero restored began almost immediately, it took until August 57 BC to secure the necessary legislation. This was due partly to intimidation by Clodius but partly also to the fact that whilst the triumvirate had not actively wished to have Cicero treated as Clodius had done – Caesar even tried to save him from it – they were prepared to use the opportunity to put strict conditions on Cicero's activities in return for their support in the moves to restore him. Cicero also regarded his position in 58 BC as having been immeasurably weakened by Clodius' bribing of the consuls Piso and Gabinius with new and lucrative proconsular provinces (respectively Macedonia and Syria). It is true that the hostility of the consuls did not help Cicero, but Clodius' bribing of them was probably aimed more at Caesar and Pompey, who had expected that the two consuls would be the protectors of their interests in 58 BC.

Against Marcus Cato, Clodius moved in a more subtle fashion. Cato had long, like Sulla, been opposed to provincial appointments of an extraordinary nature – whether because of their length or because they were bestowed on men whose lack of seniority did not justify them. Rome had recently acquired the island of Cyprus as a province; it needed organising, and

Clodius proposed that Cato, who had so far risen only to the rank of quaestor, should be given the standing of an ex-praetor in order to qualify him for the task. From Clodius' point of view, a vocal opponent was thus removed from Rome – and compromised: even Caesar appreciated the subtlety of this.

There was, however, nothing subtle about Clodius' treatment of Pompey; he was subject to attacks and humiliation by Clodius' gangs – to the extent that Pompey felt it necessary to organise his own gangs. Clodius wanted his revenge on Pompey but also needed to ensure that Pompey was effectively neutralised as a possible rival in the affections of the urban plebs. Since Pompey was forever boasting of his influence and patronage, the tactic that Clodius chose to use against him was particularly appropriate. It was undoubtedly Pompey's arrogance that led him to believe that he could not possibly be worsted by one of Clodius' standing and that therefore there was a more senior and sinister hand – probably Crassus' – behind the tribune's activities.

The question is, however, not relevant: whilst it is true that each of the triumvirate at various times hoped to use Clodius for his own ends, the fact remains that the tribune's programme was of his own construction to suit his own ambitions for dominance. Others may have benefited from individual measures, but this should be seen as incidental. In any case, Pompey's colleagues in the triumvirate had little to gain from a humiliation of the general which might lead him to rethink his alliances; the events of the next few years demonstrated this well enough.

Immediately, however, Pompey needed allies to protect him from Clodius; his own gangs could counter Clodius', but for vocal support he desired the restoration of Cicero from exile. Because of the hooliganism and corruption that were by now the prevalent features of Roman politics, it took, as we have seen, until August 57 BC to secure this, and then only after Caesar had put some kind of conditions, presumably of quiescence, on the orator's behaviour.

Cicero returned in triumph – and to two interrelated issues: first, there was a shortage of corn (caused to a large extent by Clodius' reform of the dole in 58 BC); and second, the pro-Roman (and pro-Pompeian) Ptolemy Auletes had been driven from the Egyptian throne. Egypt was a key to the grain supply and, as we have seen before, its wealth was much coveted by

Roman politicians, who saw it as a great aid to their ability to patronise. There is little doubt that Pompey wished to be entrusted with sorting out both of these problems, and it is equally clear that others – the *optimates* and Crassus – wished to avoid giving Pompey sweeping new powers. Cicero's natural inclination, now reinforced by his sense of gratitude over Pompey's part in his restoration, was to support Pompey. But he had to be cautious and diplomatic, for he needed the good-will of the *optimates* amongst the priests, who were, of course, opposed to Pompey, in the matter of seeking the deconsecration of the shrine that Clodius had had erected on the site of Cicero's house.

In the event, Cicero supported a consular motion giving Pompey control over the corn supply, but with powers far less wide than were proposed by Gaius Messius, one of the tribunes of 57 BC, who was widely believed to be Pompey's mouthpiece. The question of the restoration of Ptolemy Auletes generated much more difficulty and ill-feeling: the matter, as Cicero shows in one of his liveliest surviving letters, became the subject of raucous counter-chanting, which must have served to enhance Pompey's sense of humiliation. Cicero, too, was in a quandary, because he wished to be seen as supportive of Pompey, though one of Pompey's rivals for the Egyptian task was Publius Lentulus Spinther, one of the consuls of 57 BC, who had himself been of great help in the matter of Cicero's restoration. In the end, this matter was dropped for the moment; later the task was entrusted to Aulus Gabinius as proconsul of Syria (57–55 BC).

During the winter of 57–56 BC, Cicero's hopes were high that the final disintegration of the alliance between Pompey, Crassus and Caesar was imminent. Ever since 59 BC, voices had been raised questioning the validity of Caesar's consular legislation, and in the following years anti-Caesarian feeling had grown amongst the *optimates*, who undoubtedly viewed with some apprehension not only Caesar's success in Gaul but also the ruthlessness of which he showed himself to be capable. An additional weapon was given to Caesar's enemies by the fact that, despite the obvious necessity, he had for most of his proconsulship been acting outside the boundaries of his prov-ince. Lucius Domitius Ahenobarbus, one of the consular candi-dates for 55 BC, announced that, if elected, he would move for Caesar's recall from Gaul to face charges which, if carried, would have destroyed Caesar's career. Cicero, wishing finally to detach Pompey from Caesar, joined in to the extent of supporting the suggestion that the validity of at least the *lex Campana* should be questioned; Pompey, always a master of dissimulation and obfuscation, indicated that he would not be averse to this course of action.

Of course, Cicero misread the signs; for Pompey's move was designed not to complete Caesar's discomfiture, but to demonstrate to him that he (Pompey) was still the major influence in politics and that Caesar needed him. It was, in other words, meant to show that Pompey wanted the triumvirate renewed – but on his terms.

A new agreement was hammered out at Lucca in northern Italy in April 56 BC; the triumvirate remained a private agreement, although it was, in effect, witnessed by the one hundred or so senators who were present. On this occasion, the objectives were to achieve a visible balance between the actual powers of the three and to emasculate the opposition. Each of the three emerged from Lucca with military powers; Caesar's in Gaul were (by the *lex Pompeia-Licinia* of 55 BC) renewed for a further quinquennium, although – and this causes problems in understanding the final slide to civil war in 49 BC – it is not clear from when the renewal ran. It either ran straight on from the terminal date expressed in the *lex Vatinia* of 59 BC – that is, from 1 March 54 BC – or, alternatively, it may have run from a date in 55 BC, possibly coinciding with the passing of the *lex Trebonia* (of November 55 BC) which gave Pompey and Crassus their five-year commands in Spain and Syria respectively. Cicero, who was mortified by this turn of events, suffered the added humiliation of having to recommend these arrangements in a speech in the summer of 56 BC.

The 'destructive activities' of Cicero and Clodius were now to be reined in, so that opposition would lack obvious leadership – both verbal and physical. It is often suggested that a joint consulship in 55 BC for Pompey and Crassus was an item of the agreement. If so, Domitius Ahenobarbus was unimpressed as he continued to campaign until driven from the hustings by force early in 55 BC. It is perhaps more likely that the elections for 55 BC were even more of an orgy of violence and corruption than usual; the elections themselves, which should have been held in the summer of 56 BC, did not take place until January 55 BC. In these circumstances, Pompey and Crassus may have decided to stand with the general objective of putting an end to the confusion and the specific objective of keeping out Ahenobarbus, who continued to threaten to bring Caesar to book.

The new stability of the triumvirate was short-lived. Caesar's second quinquennium, which started with the much-publicised expeditions to Britain in 55 and 54 BC (which brought him much publicity in Rome), was marked in general by much hard-won progress and the great rising in 52 BC under Vercingetorix, which may have received some support from Caesar's enemies in Rome. In any case, Pompey could not resist striking his dominance on the arrangements by remaining in Rome and leaving his province and armies to be commanded for him by deputies (*legati*). Thus, in effect, all the triumviral armies and resources were being used to support Pompey's mastery of Rome.

Two events, in particular, however, made the slide to civil war that much more inevitable. First, in 54 BC Julia, Pompey's wife and Caesar's daughter, died. As an object of great affection to both her husband and her father, the loss of her influence was considerable. Pompey refused Caesar's offer to renew the marriage tie. Second, Crassus, whose military experience since the 70s BC had been very limited, proved no match for the Parthians, and he was killed at Carrhae in 53 BC, losing a number of legionary standards ('eagles').

Pompey, confident of dominance in Rome, continued to behave in an equivocal manner towards Caesar, and, though not doing anything that would risk an open breach, was already setting about consolidating his own position: in 53 BC, having declined Caesar's offer of a new marriage alliance, he married instead Cornelia, the daughter of the *optimate* Quintus Metellus Scipio. This sign of a *rapprochement* with the *optimates* was no accident; both Pompey and the *optimates*, particularly Cato and his friends, saw it as their most effective bulwark against Caesar. However, like many such arrangements, it was based upon mutual mistrust, rather than affection or common aims. For Pompey, Cornelia had very considerable political attraction; for not only was her father at the heart of the *optimates* but she was also the widow of Publius Crassus, who had been killed along with his father at Carrhae. The young Crassus had for a time served with Caesar in Gaul; thus Pompey hoped by the marriage not only to capture Crassus' clientage, but to make inroads into

Caesar's as well. The cynicism of the move was not unworthy of Pompey.

The violence reached its height at the opening of 52 BC. No magistrates whatever had been elected for 52 BC, and in January Clodius (a candidate for a praetorship) was murdered in a gang fight. Amidst the turmoil, a dictatorship for Pompey looked very likely; instead, with the support of Bibulus and Cato, Pompey was made sole consul; the senate had already passed the *senatus consultum ultimum*, giving Pompey special powers to restore order. Pompey's third consulship, in which in mid-year he took his new father-in-law, Metellus Scipio, as his colleague, was marked by a great deal of legislation that was very significant in the events leading up to civil war. Retroactive laws on violence and corruption were passed; further, Pompey sponsored all ten tribunes in passing a measure granting Caesar a dispensation from the normal rules governing personal presentation of candidature for office, with which, of course, Caesar had had trouble in 60 BC. The 'law of the ten tribunes' was designed to allow Caesar to pass straight from his proconsulship to a second consulship (perhaps in 48 BC) without a period as a private citizen during which he would be subject to the prosecution with which Ahenobarbus continued to threaten him. Cicero was later firmly of the view that this precipitated civil war because it gave Caesar a clear privilege, which Pompey later tried to deny. Again, Pompey obfuscated the issue by bringing in a further law which insisted on personal candidature on the part of those seeking office, and then exempting Caesar from it.

However, the law which was to cause all the difficulty in the negotiations between Caesar and Pompey in 51–50 BC was the *lex Pompeia de provinciis*. This was principally directed at diminishing corruption by interposing an interval of five years between the tenure of the consulship and the taking-up of a proconsulship; it was believed that businessmen would be less ready to finance electoral corruption if they had to wait for more than five years for a return on their investment. The interval that had to elapse before the rules enacted in this law were fully operational was to be filled by giving promagistracies to those who, like Cicero, had failed to take them at the proper time. Pompey's law superseded the *lex Sempronia* of Gaius Gracchus, which had enacted that the proconsular provinces should be determined in advance of the relevant elections.

Since it is clear that there was to be no discussion of Caesar's supersession until 1 March 50 BC, it would have been impossible to provide him with an earlier successor than one of the consuls of 49 BC. Thus, it was expected, perhaps even agreed, at Lucca, that Caesar would stay in Gaul in practice until the end of 49 BC, and on 1 January 48 BC would enter his second consulship. Now, under Pompey's new law, Caesar could be succeeded almost immediately his term of office expired, probably on 1 March 50 BC, which appears to have been the fifth anniversary of the date stated in the *lex Pompeia-Licinia* of 55 BC. It was a situation requiring, if conflict was to be avoided, a great store of goodwill between Caesar and Pompey; that commodity by 51 BC was in very short supply. A final measure of Pompey's consular year was the extension of his own Spanish command; therefore, the certainty of his own continued armed protection contrasted strongly with the parlous predicament that might be Caesar's.

The leading lights amongst the *optimates* had evidently settled on a 'battle plan', which looked the more necessary after Caesar's crushing of Vercingetorix crowned his Gallic campaigns with success; they could use their new alliance with Pompey to destroy the common enemy, Caesar, and then abandon Pompey who, it was thought, would be lost without his triumviral colleague. The cynicism of this at least matched Pompey's.

Throughout 51 BC *optimates*, with more political ambition than good sense, sought to raise the political temperature; an attempt by one of the consuls, Marcus Claudius Marcellus, to have Caesar recalled in view of the fact that the Gallic War was over met with a frosty response from Pompey and a tribunician veto. The same consul's flogging of a man from Cisalpine Gaul was a calculated insult to Caesar, who had tried to arrange the full enfranchisement of the area. Finally, in September, Pompey met Caesar, and returned saying that there should be no discussion of Caesar's position until 1 March 50 BC but that after that date 'he would not hesitate'.

Our knowledge of the last months of peace is greatly enhanced by the fact that Cicero, who was having to spend 51–50 BC in a proconsulship of Cilicia, secured the services of an astute observer of the political scene as his eyes and ears – Marcus Caelius Rufus, many of whose letters to Cicero survive. In these letters we see Pompey as the source of responses, which were meant to be conciliatory to Caesar, but which lacked substance;

for example, the 'compromise' proposal that Caesar should disarm on 13 November would have meant a closing of the gap between leaving the proconsulship and entering the second consulship, but would be useless to Caesar because a gap would still remain in which he could be attacked. The nub of the matter was that Caesar could not feel safe in leaving his province without his army, whilst Pompey could not feel safe so long as Caesar kept his army. Without some measure of trust, there could be no bridging this gap.

Caesar's corner in Rome was fought by one of the tribunes of 50 BC – Gaius Scribonius Curio, an *optimate* who suddenly changed sides after his election to the tribunate. Despite attempts by Caesar's enemies to argue that tribunician vetos were invalid against the moves to dispossess Caesar, Curio persisted with his throughout the year.

Cicero returned from Cilicia in November and saw, as he himself said, that he had entered a 'madhouse of men thirsting for war'. And so it seemed, though the warmongers were in fact a small, but vocal and influential, minority, as was demonstrated when on 1 December Curio called for a vote on his proposal that Pompey and Caesar should surrender their provinces *simultaneously* and the senate passed this by 370 votes to 22. The measure was immediately vetoed by a tribune acting for the 22, and Gaius Claudius Marcellus, one of the consuls of 50 BC, called on Pompey to save the republic.

Pompey's acceptance was the penultimate step before civil war; two of the new tribunes of 49 BC, Antonius and Cassius, represented Curio's disarmament proposal on 1 January, but this was countered by a move to declare Caesar a 'public enemy' (*hostis*). Antonius and Cassius were advised to leave, and the senate, despite its earlier expression of a desire for peace, passed the *senatus consultum ultimum*. Caesar now felt himself left with no alternative; with his army he crossed the river Rubicon, the stream separating his province from Italy, and so the civil war had begun. In two senses, Caesar could argue that he was fighting for the traditional rights of the tribunes – the ten who, in 52 BC, had granted him his dispensation, and the two (Antonius and Cassius) whose veto had been set aside. Ultimately, Caesar argued that he was fighting for his status (*dignitas*) and the integrity of his career. It was the *optimates* who had forced him to fight; as he observed later, the civil war was their wish.

The *optimates* made out that they had gone to war to save the republic from the dominance of individuals; many Romans, such as Cicero, agonised over which side they should join. After some four months of deliberation, he joined Pompey and the *optimates*, but rapidly came to see that there was little honour in their cause; the *optimates* were mostly bigots who looked no further than restoring the republic as their own preserve for the pursuance of their ancestral ambitions and dividing between them the spoils that they anticipated would fall to them in the wake of victory.

The war went on in various theatres of the empire until 45 BC, but the decisive battle was fought at Pharsalus in Greece in 48 BC. Pompey and the *optimates* had quit Italy early in 49 BC, not so much to save the land from the ravages of war as to establish bases that were close to the wealth and clientage in Asia Minor, which Pompey hoped would win the war for him, and to stretch Caesar's lines of supply and communication. Pompey was decisively beaten at Pharsalus, and some 30,000 of his men were killed or captured; he himself escaped to Egypt, seeking refuge with the son of Ptolemy Auletes. However, the young Ptolemy and his sister, Cleopatra, were more concerned to propitiate the rising than the setting sun; to this end they had Pompey murdered – an abject end for a man who, despite his uncongenial political performance, had achieved a great deal for Rome in the empire.

For Caesar and those who survived, there was little space for triumph; for them, the priorities were reconciliation and the reconstruction of the shattered republic.

8

Caesar's dictatorship

The civil war had split families and friends apart, as they tried to weigh the rights and wrongs, the advantages and disadvantages, of the two sides. Cicero's friend Caelius Rufus chose Caesar because he thought Caesar would win; Cicero, although he had developed a personal affection for Caesar in the later 50s BC, joined Pompey out of loyalty and because, for him, Pompey's alliance with the *optimates* offered hope that it was the 'better side'. But, as Syme observed in *The Roman Revolution* (p.59), liberty and the republic were high-sounding words; in practice, however, they meant little more than the maintenance of the privileges and vested interests of the *optimate* nobility.

Caesar's supporters in the civil war were a disparate group: the army, the urban plebs, equestrians, patrician families long depressed politically and financially who saw in Caesar's rise an opportunity for themselves, and senators, particularly younger ones, who felt alienated by the bigotry of the leading *optimates*; some of Caesar's supporters were plain adventurers, whilst others joined him out of personal affection. We should not lose sight of the fact that, although Caesar could be harsh to his enemies and intolerant of opposition, there was a degree of personal loyalty and magnetism in him which contrasted strongly with the cynical manoeuvring of the *optimates*, particularly of Cato and his friends. Cicero, as we have seen, found the choice difficult to make, and this was not least because he remembered the care and loyalty that characterised Caesar's relationship with his (Cicero's) temperamental brother, Quintus, in Gaul.

A major problem, however, was that whilst such a disparate faction as Caesar's was relatively easy to hold together in war, its wide variety of expectations made this much harder in peacetime; then, the breadth of Caesar's support could become a liability. Another serious difficulty for Caesar when he set out for war, but even more so as he embarked upon post-war reconstruction, was caused by the fact that the great luminaries of the republic, the noble families, had generally joined Pompey. This inevitably made Caesar stand out above his faction in a way that many interpreted as increasingly 'monarchic'; Caesar was himself sensitive about this, as is shown by his famous response that he was 'not king, but Caesar'.

After the Pompeian defeat at Pharsalus in 48 BC, whilst some of Pompey's supporters vowed to fight on, many were eager to seize the opportunity to put war behind them and resume a more normal life. Caesar's attitude to defeated enemies was generous; he had, after all, long made a virtue of his kindness (*clementia*) in such circumstances, and he knew that if he was to succeed in bringing peace and stability he would have to carry with him a good proportion of his defeated enemies. Not that stability would be easy to achieve, for wounds had gone deep. The example of Cicero illustrates this poignantly; Cicero's brother, who had served with Caesar in Gaul but who joined his brother on Pompey's side in the civil war, now sought Caesar's clemency, by arguing that it was his brother's fault, not his, that he had attached himself to the wrong side .

Caesar knew that it was not sufficient merely to hope that, after the war, the peace would look after itself; for Julius Caesar was one of a relatively rare breed amongst Roman aristocrats – one who actually *thought* about the needs of government. Nor was his thinking, like Cicero's, largely on a theoretical level. He was one of the first Romans to give active consideration to the methods by which Rome and Italy could sit at the centre of a well-ordered, well-defended and prosperous empire. He had already shown his care for this by a new law on extortion which he had brought in during his first consulship (59 BC), and more recently by his liberal treatment of defeated Gauls, leaving them free of the ravages of Roman tax collectors by introducing the concepts of tax assessement and local responsibility for collection, and offering them the opportunities inherent in grants of Roman citizenship. This was the *pax Romana* of Augustus Caesar in embryonic form.

Caesar also recognised the problems of domestic politics, in particular the increasing ungovernability of the republic as individual and factional ambitions promoted themselves using the opportunities of wealth and military power which the growing empire had brought in its wake. 'The republic', Caesar is reported to have observed, 'is a mere name, without form or substance.' This was not the contemptuous judgement that it is often made out to have been, but simply an observation implying that there was nothing 'sacred' in the way government was carried out in the early days and that it should be capable of adaptation to meet changing situations.

This led Caesar, as it led Cicero too, to contemplate ways of preserving as much as possible of governmental tradition, whilst lending to it the means to achieve stability. As we have seen, Cicero had hoped that his 'union of the orders', under the benevolent guidance of a figure of standing, would provide an answer. Pompey's death had naturally removed him from Cicero's considerations, but there is evidence to suggest that, by 47–46 BC, Cicero was finding renewed hope in a *concordia* 'moderated' by Julius Caesar. Of course, Cicero's hopes had been born of specific events and circumstances; Caesar, it appears, had thought more broadly on the same topics. His remark that 'Sulla only showed his foolishness by resigning his dictatorship' indicates that Caesar's thinking was now embracing the notion of permanent supervision of the republic – a logical and realistic development perhaps, but one which many members of the Roman nobility would have found painful to contemplate.

Caesar's task was to put the republic in order; to do this, he had to find the means of making his kind of thinking broadly acceptable. Of course, those who looked to Caesar as their patron would find little difficulty with this, but convincing defeated enemies, and even reluctant friends, was another matter. Many of those who returned to Rome after the debacle of Pharsalus were sufficiently eager for peace to contemplate the necessity of temporary supervision of the republic by Caesar, until such time as wounds were healed; Cicero was amongst these, and he might have gone further had events not demonstrated to him at least that Caesar's supervision represented a slippery slope to autocracy.

Caesar meant his period of power to represent a new start for the republic – a phoenix rising from the ashes of civil war. From the start, he thought it necessary to emphasise his control: the basis of it was the dictatorship which he held for varying periods from 49 BC and which became 'perpetual' in 44 BC. It is important to make the point that by this latter move Caesar was not necessarily becoming dictator forever, but that he was holding the office for an indefinite period without the statement of a terminal date when, in republican tradition, he could be called to account for his tenure. This may have been an illustration of poor judgement on Caesar's part, but it also shows his view that the supervision the republic required stretched into a longer-term future. The great advantages of the dictatorship for Caesar were that the *imperium* of the office was 'superior' to that of other magistracies and, because the tradition of the office was rooted in national emergencies, it carried immunity from the tribunician veto.

Caesar was also consul in 48 BC and from 46 to 44 BC; indeed, in 45 he was sole consul, as Pompey had been in 52 BC. Caesar's holding of this office may have been intended as a cloak of 'republican normality'; alternatively, he may have been trying to restrict the number of *nobiles* reaching the office. There is no real evidence that he contemplated a *transitio ad plebem*, after the manner of Clodius, in order to become a tribune, though in 44 BC he was given a special grant of tribunician inviolability (*sacrosanctitas*). Since 63 BC, Caesar had been chief priest and in 47 BC he became an *augur*: these offices provided him with a strong control over the religious activity of the republic, with all the opportunity of political manoeuvring that attached to the state religion. It is clear, too, that Caesar enjoyed certain censorial powers – over the senate's membership and over the republic's moral and social fabric. These powers, in addition to his military role and his widespread patronage, meant that he exercised a dominant position over the government of the republic.

The extent of his powers was, of course, a significant indicator of Caesar's view of the republic; it is important to see where this left the traditional organs of government. The popular assemblies were well on their way to becoming ciphers; Caesar's widespread patronage of equestrians, plebs and armies saw to this. The senate, too, changed its appearance during his period of power. Whilst the stories of Caesar's wish to fill the senate with 'trousered Gauls' were clearly exaggerated, he did have a view of the senate that to some degree broke with the past. Although, like any victorious leader, he had supporters who required rewards in status, there is evidence too that on a small scale at least Caesar saw the efficacy of making the senate's membership more broadly representative than of Rome and Italy alone. Caesar was, in fact, moving in a direction that his great admirer, the emperor Claudius (AD 41–54), tried to emulate; removing those areas of power, such as finance and foreign policy, which the senate had itself usurped from the *populus*, Caesar hoped to make the senate more of a consultative body. The problem was that, with its numbers increased to 900 mainly with Caesar's supporters, it was easy to treat this senate as a 'rubber stamp'. Cicero, indeed, complained of an occasion when he found his name added to the signatories to a senatorial decree although he had not even been present at the meeting.

Caesar's attitude to magistracies was equally cavalier: he did not abolish elections, but the extent of his patronage ensured that they became a formality. The numbers of annual magistrates were increased both to reward and to ensure a sufficient supply of men for the jobs involved. On some occasions, however, elections were postponed (for example, in 47 and 45 BC) and the administrative affairs handed temporarily at least to 'prefects' (*praefecti*) of Caesar's own choosing. There is no doubt that all of this was seen by many as a serious departure from traditional arrangements and an elimination of traditional opportunities. Caesar had long had a tendency to be intolerant of opposition, but this drive to efficiency was bound to heighten opposition rather than allay it.

Much that Caesar did or planned was directed at achieving a harmonious empire with Rome at the centre, an imperial city worthy of the name. Attention was given to improving the financial and governmental lot of the provinces over the empire as a whole along the lines that he had adumbrated in Gaul. Colonies of his veterans and of other citizens from Rome were planted across the empire to enhance security and stability, and local people were offered opportunities to participate in local administration; further, the fact that these measures enhanced trade, as was intended, meant that at local level men had the opportunity to prosper and thus qualify for local administrative office, and that the treasury in Rome would thereby benefit from an improved tax take.

Caesar greatly reduced the numbers of those in Rome receiving the corn dole, partly because, unlike Cicero, he believed it demoralising and dangerous and partly, too, because he preferred to create jobs by which people could buy their necessities and thus increase trade. Thus, he initiated a huge programme of prestigious buildings, such as his public hall (*basilica Iulia*) and public square and 'business park' (*forum Iulium*), which was crowned with a temple to Venus Genetrix, the tutelary deity of the Julian family. In addition, schemes were put in hand to relieve the flooding of the Tiber and to ensure the upkeep of roads, together with the draining of the Pomptine Marshes and the reconstruction of Rome's harbour at Ostia. This was an expensive programme, but one which could be in part paid for by the proceeds from Caesar's wars, by savings on the corn dole and by some increased taxation. It may also be that Caesar's renewed interest in Egypt from 47 BC onwards was at least partly directed towards control of Egypt's wealth.

Throughout most of his period of power Caesar was involved in warfare; some of this was the continuance of the civil war under surviving *optimate* leaders and Pompey's sons. But it is evident too that, like Augustus later, Caesar was planning the kind of warfare that would keep his troops employed in lucrative campaigning as well as securing frontiers that would offer a better defence for the empire – for example, on the Danube and in the east, in both of which theatres attention was necessary.

However, the vibrancy and vigour of much of Caesar's activity cut little ice with those *optimates* with whom Caesar was trying to work in Rome and even with men, like Cicero, who had attempted to give Caesar a chance. Republicanism and Caesarism were polarised, however, by the suicide in north Africa in 46 BC of Marcus Cato. His death, that of a martyr for the republican cause, pricked the conscience of many who had tried to work with Caesar. Pamphlets appeared in praise of Cato, a man who died true to his principles; rather than let such ephemeral literature pass, Caesar unwisely released a counterblast in the form of an 'anti-Cato', which proved counterproductive in that it heightened the perception of antithesis between the two men, which was still momentous three years later when the historian, Sallust, wrote his account of the Catilinarian conspiracy of 63 BC. The climax of Sallust's work was a debate on the fate of the conspirators in which pride of place was given to the orations of Caesar and Cato. In 63 BC Cato had thundered against the would-be wreckers of the republic; in 46 BC, Cato decided that he could no longer bear the travesty of Caesar's republic. From this point on, Caesar's assassination was inevitable.

What, then, were the aims of the conspirators against Caesar? It is clear that Caesar was the victim of a campaign of disinformation: despite the allegations, there is no serious evidence that Caesar wished to elevate himself to the level of divinity. His behaviour in this regard did not go beyond the normal practice of Roman commanders, who tolerated adulation in the east, where it was a natural feature of political life to treat leaders as gods. There is no evidence that he wished to live with Cleopatra, move the capital to Alexandria, reign like a Hellenistic monarch and bequeath his kingdom to Caesarion, his and Cleopatra's son. This is likely to have been an exaggerated interpretation of Caesar's fascination with Cleopatra and his concern to do what was necessary to retain the availability to himself of the wealth of Egypt. Nor is there evidence to suggest that Caesar wished to be king in Rome; indeed, it is clear that he was aware of and sensitive to this charge, and wished to counter it. The stage-managed occasion when Caesar refused Antonius' offer of a golden crown was such an attempt. The campaign of disinformation was intended by Caesar's enemies to isolate the *dictator* and to justify what they were conspiring to do. There is, in fact, some similarity between the tactics of Caesar's opponents and those of Tiberius Gracchus' enemies in 133 BC.

The domination of Caesar and his faction, of which Antonius and Lepidus were the principal members, was as thoroughgoing as anything seen in Rome since Sulla's time; as with the example of Sulla, the personality of Caesar as the leader was projected before the people through the coinage. Nor is there any evidence that the mass of the population had any objection to this. The conspirators, on the other hand, were drawn from the senatorial aristocracy and resented the way in which the traditional organs of republican government had been reduced to almost total dependence upon Caesar; they resented, too (perhaps even more), the fact that their traditional freedom to pursue their careers in the public service had suffered from Caesar's interference. Such interference was domination, and Caesar's well-known generosity to opponents (*clementia*) in a way served to emphasise this. For *dominatio* described the relationship between master and slave, and *clementia* was a characteristic of such a relationship because the granting or withholding of it was subject not to laws, but to the whim of the master.

Brutus, Cassius and the others who, like Cicero, attached themselves to the conspiracy acted less out of enmity to Caesar than out of a desire to destroy his *dominatio*. However, as had been the case with Cicero and his view of Catiline in 63 BC, this group naively believed that all would be well as a result of removing the tyrant; they were not planning a revolution. There were no plans to control the organs of government in the aftermath of assassination, because the conspirators saw no need to do this. In the event, they removed the tyrant, and left a vacuum.

It is plain from Cicero's correspondence that in the last year or so before his death Caesar was becoming increasingly depressed about his inability to offer an acceptable route to stability in government. He needed to control the ambitions of the nobility but at the same time leave them feeling that they could still fulfil their ambitions. Brutus is a good illustration of the problem that Caesar faced: he joined Pompey and the *optimates* in the civil war, partly out of conviction but perhaps partly too out of class loyalty; after Pharsalus, he returned to Italy seemingly reconciled to Caesar, and had reached the praetorship in 44 BC. Yet plainly he could see no future for *libertas* under the patronage of Caesar.

Few amongst the nobility, probably, doubted the essential decency of Caesar; to Gaius Cassius, he was *clemens dominus* – a generous patron, but a *dominus* (master) none the less. Caesar, in other words, partly because of his personality and partly perhaps because of the circumstances of his coming to power, could not provide a form of government acceptable to the *optimates*. As one of Caesar's non-political friends was later to write in a letter to Cicero, 'for all his genius, Caesar could not find a way out'.

Yet, to understand the aftermath, we have to bear in mind that the *libertas* for which Brutus and Cassius struck Caesar down on the Ides (15th) of March 44 BC meant very little to the mass of the population. The people, the armies, the equestrians and even some senators were coming to experience that sense of dependence upon the factional and national leader (*princeps*) that was to be a feature of the Augustan *principate*. When Cicero talked of Brutus, Cassius and the conspirators being protected by the devoted loyalty of all Italy, he showed his failure to grasp the real pulse of the *respublica*. However, his own realisation that the problem was greater than simply the removal of the tyrant is soon seen as Marcus Antonius, consul in 44 BC, asserted the continuing control of the Caesarian faction after the assassination; the broadly based appeal of Antonius was, for most, a more intelligible approach than the arcane traditions to which the likes of Brutus and Cassius appealed. Yet Cicero's rather tasteless comment, that 'the banquet of the Ides of March was short by one course' (that is, Marcus Antonius), shows that he was as far away as ever from understanding the realities of politics, and the *respublica* remained in deep trouble.

9

The final act
Antonius, Octavian and Lepidus

As we have seen, the initiative, after Caesar's murder, did not long remain with the conspirators. Whilst they took refuge from popular anger, the surviving consul, Marcus Antonius, who, despite a frankly undistinguished early career, had been well enough regarded by Caesar to be treated as his 'deputy', took full advantage of the confusion to assert the continuing domination of the Caesarian faction with himself as its new leader; other Caesarians, such as Marcus Lepidus, were persuaded to support Antonius. Claiming to use Caesar's will, Antonius made himself the centre of patronage, offered some concessions to republican sentiment, including an amnesty for the conspirators in return for the survival of Caesar's legislative measures (*acta*), and thus claimed responsibility for the return of ordered government. He also ensured that after his consulship he would receive the lucrative province of Macedonia, thus inheriting the military plans that Caesar had laid in the east. Republicans, like Cicero, might rail at this, but with little political, and less military, muscle, there was little that they could do about it; Antonius had gambled, and apparently succeeded.

The difficulties of Caesar's deputy, however, emanated from a much less obvious source. In his last months, Caesar had adopted as his son and heir his great-nephew, Gaius Octavius, and enrolled the eighteen-year-old amongst the patricians. This obscure young man, whom Caesar had treated as a son for some

88

years, thus became Gaius Julius Caesar Octavianus; although for clarity's sake we refer to him as Octavian, he disliked this part of his adoptive nomenclature and, for obvious reasons, preferred to style himself 'Caesar'.

When Julius Caesar was assassinated, Octavian was in the Balkans, waiting with his young friend, Marcus Agrippa, to join Caesar on his planned eastern expedition: it was intended to be the first step on an 'apprenticeship' that would in time lead them both to senatorial careers. Octavian was back in Italy by April; not surprisingly, he did not find Antonius particularly helpful. Caesar's deputy was bitter about the position of Caesar's heir and was clearly in no mood to treat him on equal terms. Nor, in one sense, was this unreasonable, since Antonius was consul and, according to Sulla's rules, Octavian should have expected to have to wait for nearly a quarter of a century more to reach that position. Unwisely, Antonius was dismissive, saying publicly that Octavian 'owed everything to his name', but at the same time he reorganised the proconsular provinces for 43 BC, giving up Macedonia (though retaining its army) and receiving instead a five-year command of Cisalpine and Transalpine Gaul. This might be regarded as a rash reminder of Caesar's position in the late 50s BC.

Caesar's friends and veterans, however, welcomed the new Caesar; republicans, like Cicero, began to see Octavian as an ally against Antonius, rather unwisely reviving the plan that Cato had originally inspired for playing off Pompey and Caesar against each other in the late 50s BC. Octavian was using his own resources to appeal to Caesar's veterans and even won over two of Antonius' legions; Cicero, highly flattered that the 'divine youth' should choose to sit at his feet, began to entertain the possibility that Octavian might be persuaded to guard the *concordia ordinum*, and thus fulfil the role that Pompey and Caesar had ignored. In a new confidence, Cicero thundered out his series of 'Philippic orations' against Antonius, seeking at every turn to undermine the credibility of the man who was aiming at dictatorship and was more to be feared even than Julius Caesar. Even Brutus and Cassius, who were busy suborning the troops of pro-Antonius proconsuls in the east, became worried at the obsessive exclusiveness of Cicero's vituperations.

Cicero's plan was that at the end of 44 BC Antonius should be denied access to the province of which he was the legally appointed *proconsul*, that the senate should support Decimus Brutus, Antonius' predecessor in that province and one of the conspirators against Caesar, in a refusal to give way, and that an army should be sent north to defeat Antonius, headed by Hirtius and Pansa, the consuls of 43 BC; further, Octavian was to be given a special grant of propraetorian *imperium* to qualify him for a commanding role in this expedition. For the second time in his career, Cicero was proposing that the republic should set aside its laws to defeat an enemy in the name of some higher, and ill-defined, justice.

Antonius, who besieged Decimus Brutus at Mutina (modern Modena), was defeated, but escaped. In the event, it appears more than possible that this was allowed to happen by the collusive connivance of Lepidus and Octavian. In the fighting, the consuls had been killed, leaving Octavian as *de facto* commander of the republic's whole army. Instructed by Cicero and the senate to hand these troops over to the senior republican commander in the area (Decimus Brutus), Octavian refused, arguing now that he could not be expected to co-operate with a man who had had a hand in the assassination of his adoptive father; the 'divine youth' was already displaying a great maturity in political cynicism. Instead, he marched his eight legions on Rome, demanded (and received) a consulship from a senate that now presumably appreciated the gravity of its misjudgement, and straightaway returned north to meet Antonius and Lepidus.

The result of the meeting was the formation of the second triumvirate. This was not an informal, private, arrangement after the manner of that between Pompey, Crassus and Caesar; rather, it was an organ of government, sanctified in law, with the task of stabilising the republic. Thus, the single dictator, assassinated on 15 March 44 BC, was on 27 November 43 BC replaced in effect (but not in title) by three. They divided the west between them, a division which by its nature clearly marked out Antonius as the senior partner and which left Octavian with the 'maritime' provinces of Africa, Sicily and Sardinia – which would be difficult to control in view of the piratical activities of Pompey's surviving son, Sextus, who was based on Sicily and styling himself in grandiose fashion the 'son of Neptune'. Despite the formal 'job description' of the triumvirate, the triple personality cult on the coinage, as well as the conduct of the three, made it abundantly clear that the republic, for which Brutus and Cassius had assassinated Caesar, was dead.

The immediate task of the new triumvirate, which was made up of three men who ostensibly derived their political credentials from Julius Caesar, was to lead the Caesarian faction in avenging its dead leader's murder. To do this, they needed money to pay troops and settle veterans, and whilst away in the east they needed to have confidence in political stability in Rome and Italy. The solution to both necessities was the instigation of a new programme of proscriptions after the model introduced by Sulla; although the programme had some prominent victims, including (predictably) Cicero, the clear majority came from the equestrian order, indicating that money was the chief priority.

As a result, by the summer of 42 BC the three could put forty-three legions into the field to match the nineteen that Brutus and Cassius had acquired by fairly dubious means in the east, and which they maintained by the results of their rapacity in Asia Minor. The political heirs of Caesar had in effect to repeat what Caesar had himself had to do in 49–48 BC – take on with stretched supply-lines an enemy that had considerable resources close at hand. The conclusive battles at Philippi in Greece in the autumn of 42 BC were effectively won by Antonius; Lepidus had been left to keep order in Italy, and Octavian proved too ill to participate. The defeat drove Brutus and Cassius to suicide; of their supporters, some joined the *triumviri*, whilst others, particularly those most implacably opposed to Caesarism, took refuge with Sextus Pompeius on Sicily. Thus, the avenging of Caesar's murder was complete.

In the aftermath of the battle, a new territorial division took place. Antonius received Gaul and the east, where it was intended that he would acquire funds for settlement of veterans; Lepidus was at first given nothing, on the ground that he was aiding and abetting Sextus Pompeius, but was later to receive Africa; Octavian, who had since Caesar's deification been entitled to style himself *divi filius* ('son of god'), received Spain, Italy and the islands, as well as Africa. Without doubt, Octavian had been given the most difficult and dangerous post-war task, for he had to handle Sextus Pompeius and mastermind a huge programme of land confiscation, mainly in Italy, in order to discharge all but eleven of the triumviral legions. It is tolerably clear that Antonius had hoped and expected that his colleague would be totally submerged in the unpopularity that would attend such a programme and, to make sure, had primed his wife and brother to exacerbate Octavian's problems.

Octavian survived all of this and defeated his opponents at the town of Perusia (modern Perugia), showing little mercy, but pardoning Antonius' brother. Octavian's successful surmounting of this crisis brought Antonius back to Italy and a new agreement, the treaty of Brundisium (40 BC). By this the earlier territorial division was adjusted, adding Gaul to Octavian's command and giving Africa to Lepidus; the agreement was sealed by a marriage between the recently widowed Antonius and Octavian's sister, Octavia. In a manner that looks forward to aspects of Augustan succession policy, it may have been hoped that a union between the deputy leader of Caesar's party and the family of Caesar's heir would itself produce an heir that would draw the whole Caesarian faction together – as when, some twenty years later, Augustus arranged a marriage between his friend Agrippa and his daughter, Julia.

The ensuing decade, the last before the battle of Actium (31 BC) and the emergence of Octavian unrivalled in primacy, was dominated by the polarisation of the positions and support of Antonius and Octavian. Antonius was by now preoccupied with the problems of the east, including his relationship with Cleopatra, whilst Octavian, despite difficulties, consolidated his dominance of the west. This enabled him increasingly to present himself as the centre of a network of patronage for politicians, financiers and literary figures. The respectability that went with this enabled Octavian to begin to draw a veil across the excesses of the early triumviral years; it was a respectability that was enhanced by the fact that, as the members of his faction themselves grew in stature, he was able to emphasise the role of himself and his faction in stabilising peace, security and prosperity in the west. He was thus able increasingly to use his own well-developed demagogic skills and his control of propaganda to show that he was the defender, indeed the embodiment, of all that was best in Roman and Italian tradition.

By contrast, that same propaganda machine was able to minimise the undoubted successes of Antonius in the east, emphasise his difficulties (as when, in 36 BC, one of his generals, Decidius Saxa, lost further prestige to the Parthians), and play on the untraditional dalliance with Cleopatra, and the plans, real or supposed, that the two had for the future of the Roman world. Not only that, but Octavian, who had adequately shown in 44–43 BC the pliability of his principles, was able to stand as the moral paragon rebuking Antonius for defiling the honour of Octavia. Thus, events enabled Octavian to put the integrity of traditional Italian political and family life at the top of his programme.

There were, of course, difficulties along the way, though on more than one occasion Octavian displayed an adept skill at grabbing success out of difficulty. For example, soon after the treaty of Brundisium, Sextus Pompeius, annoyed at having been ignored, increased his piratical activities. A new accord between him and the three signed at Misenum (near Naples) in 39 BC, not only (temporarily at least) satisfied Sextus Pompeius, but also allowed the large number of senatorial families whose loyalty to the republic had led them to take refuge with the son of Pompey to return to Italy. Members of senior *optimate* families, whose opposition to Julius Caesar had been intense, could now re-enter public life under the patronage of the new Caesar. This was important for it saved Octavian from the danger, which had proved so serious for Caesar, of being surrounded by men who socially (and thus politically) were of small account.

As if to symbolise his new understanding with the luminaries of the republic, Octavian, in circumstances which some thought scandalous, divorced his wife, Scribonia, and married Livia Drusilla, herself the wife of Tiberius Claudius Nero, an erstwhile supporter and latterly bitter opponent of Julius Caesar. Livia and Tiberius Nero already had one son (the future emperor Tiberius), and Livia was pregnant again at the time of her divorce and re-marriage. She was recommended not just by the social respectability of her husband but also by the blood of the Livii Drusi and the patrician Claudii Pulchri that she carried in her veins.

Relations between Octavian and Sextus Pompeius did not improve for long, and in 37 BC, at Tarentum, the triumvirate, which had formally lapsed at the end of the previous year, was renewed for a further five years. The help that Octavian received from Antonius in the form of 120 ships enabled him, through the agency of Agrippa, now his senior commander, to take on Sextus Pompeius and defeat him in 36 BC. A bizarre, but dangerous, attempt by Lepidus to reassert himself and claim

Sicily was thwarted by Octavian's presenting himself to the troops as 'Caesar'; the name still served to inspire loyalty and obedience. Lepidus, for his trouble, was stripped of his triumviral title and left to live out his days as *pontifex maximus* in Africa.

The defeat of Sextus Pompeius was proclaimed as the establishment of peace; Octavian's generals, acting under the auspices of *imperator Caesar*, had defeated their enemies on land and at sea. As if themselves looking to the normalities of life in peacetime, the plebs granted to Octavian the personal inviolability of a tribune; like Caesar, of course, Octavian was a patrician and thus was ineligible to hold the office of tribune. Other signs of peace were in the air: the settlement of veteran colonies in Italy and the provinces, the beginnings of restoration of the temples of the traditional gods, and the physical enhancement of Rome and Italy with buildings intended for the purposes of entertainment and relaxation, promoting business life, and striking a suitable tone for a successful imperial city. All of this was viewed in Rome as being in marked contrast to the more equivocal record of Marcus Antonius. In particular, his 'Donations of Alexandria' in 34 BC made a bad impression; in these arrangements, he divided the east between his and Cleopatra's children, proclaimed Cleopatra as 'queen of kings' and announced that Caesarion was Caesar's true heir, thus implying the illegitimacy of Octavian's claim to that title.

Octavian's propaganda machine was able to make much of this, but we may ask how outrageous it really was. Placing territory into the hands of friendly monarchs (client kings) was to become a regular feature of overseas policy under the emperors and had already been used to a certain extent in Rome's dealings with Asia Minor. At no time did Antonius claim for himself an eastern title, though he did attract many of the visible signs of eastern monarchy; he continued to justify his activities by his triumviral power, and coins issued in the east as late as 32–31 BC, commemorating each of the legions, proclaimed him as 'Antonius, Augur, *Triumvir* for the stabilising of the republic'. It is also worth noting that when, in 32 BC, the final battle-lines were being drawn between Antonius and Octavian, both the consuls in Rome, together with some 300 senators, left Rome to join Antonius in Greece.

The triumviral agreement lapsed at the end of 33 BC; this time

Octavian needed no renewal. He was the head of a successful faction; consulships and proconsulships went to his supporters; he proclaimed himself the defender of traditional standards in national and family life. In the last months before war, Italian communities swore an oath of allegiance to him personally as leader; in this way, the whole of Italy effectively became part of his clientage, and his standing (*auctoritas*) rose immeasurably as a result. Although Octavian might try to portray the looming conflict as a righteous war in which traditional standards were being defended against the onslaught of oriental barbarism, the truth was otherwise. The battle of Actium, off the Greek coast, in 31 BC, was the final act in a struggle for dominance between rival faction leaders. In essence, therefore, it differed little from the factional crises that had been a regular feature of Roman political life since the mid-second century BC.

The victory that Agrippa won for Octavian in 31 BC set the final seal on the old republic; by 30 BC, both Antonius and Cleopatra were dead, and Octavian (the new Caesar) was the undisputed master of the Roman world, the victorious faction leader. The struggle in Roman politics between the primacy of the traditional forms of government and the domination of factional and individual ambition had finally been settled.

Epilogue

Historians have seen the battle of Actium as a watershed – the end of the republic and the beginning of the Augustan *principate*. It is doubtful whether most Romans would have been aware of this great milestone, as Octavian, his faction and patronage represented a massive demonstration of continuity. Because of this, it was easy for such slogans as 'the restored republic' (*respublica restituta*) to slip into the political vocabulary.

In a sense, of course, Octavian's victory at Actium was not the fall of the republic, but a decisive stage in its evolution – decisive, because the Augustan *principate* that followed proved to be the way of supervising the *respublica* that had previously been so elusive. The evolution – some would say collapse – of the Roman republic had in fact been a process continuing and gathering momentum over at least the century before Actium. The traditional governmental instruments of the republic did not disappear but went on to be essential parts of the Augustan *principate*.

The change that characterised the gradual fall of the republic lay in the relationship between the instruments of government and the manner in which they worked. Their original forms had suited the needs of a small city-state with few external interests or responsibilities; they suited, too, a state in which it was thought perfectly appropriate that a relatively small group of

96

people should, because of the contribution that their wealth enabled them to make, enjoy a virtual monopoly of power.

The concentration of power into the hands of a small oligarchic group did not change; its stability, however, was disturbed by the opportunities offered by a growing empire for members of this group to pursue individual visions and ambitions. Thus, individuals and factions came to see that they could exploit the republic's forms for their own needs, and at the expense of their peers. The means by which this could be done changed with time, but a decisive point was undoubtedly reached when these factions and individuals could count armies and kings amongst their clients. From then on, the fact that political and military power was vested in the same people made disorder and anarchy inevitable.

Many were obsessed simply with capitalising on this state of affairs; a few tried to find a way in which stability could be maintained, realised that the supervision of the republic had to be achieved, and saw that this was realistically open only to those who controlled the military power. The crudeness of approach exemplified by men like the Gracchi, Scipio Aemilianus, Marius, Catiline or Clodius proved intolerable to their peers; the openly authoritarian stances of Sulla and Caesar seemed for a while to offer hope, but, in the event, the hope was illusory because their domination removed from their peers a genuine opportunity to compete for honours and fulfil ambitions.

A voice that might have pointed a way through the *impasse* was that of Cicero; in his 'union of the orders' he recognised the need for a stability based upon a certain type of harmony and upon an ultimate guarantee of armed protection for that harmony. Perhaps because he was an Italian rather than a Roman, Cicero's vision was broader than most Romans could embrace, though it still lacked the breadth of a man like Julius Caesar, who took into account not only the ordinary people of Rome, for whom Cicero had little concern, but also the empire at large. Ultimately, Cicero was too constrained by the system, as is demonstrated by the fact that his great moments of effectiveness (63 and 44–43 BC) coincided with behaviour on his part that was in legal terms outrageous.

Cicero was, however, right in at least one important respect: the nobility would not tolerate obvious and institutional domination, and so control had to be exercised in a more subtle manner. Although there is no suggestion that Augustus – the honorific name that Octavian was granted in 27 BC – modelled his *principate* on Ciceronian principles, he did share Cicero's appreciation that supervision had to be exercised with subtlety. For political and personal reasons, Pompey was an inappropriate choice on Cicero's part, but Cicero was right in believing that the *moderator* should be able to exercise his role through the strength of his personality, clientage and standing in the republic (*auctoritas*), rather than by virtue of any specific office that he might hold. Augustus' second settlement of the *principate* (23 BC) approached the problem in a not dissimilar way.

In this he based his own control on the tribunician power (*tribunicia potestas*) and an overriding military power (*imperium proconsulare maius*), though in practical terms he was neither a tribune nor a *proconsul*. He thus demonstrated his appreciation of where the seeds of the republic's management (and mismanagement) lay. He appreciated, too, the need for a broad harmony; senators and equestrians were brought together as the two arms of a governmental and imperial service. Honours were open to competition, and elections were held as normal; Augustus' influence was exercised through a traditional form of canvassing which, because of his standing, was sufficient and successful. Thus, magistrates and promagistrates were dependent upon him, but not in an overt or humiliating fashion. Further, Augustus' control of the army was exercised through trusted individuals who emerged by means of this system.

Augustus was concerned too to occupy a traditional patronal role with regard to ordinary people; his building programmes provided work, and there was food and entertainment available to the urban plebs. Provincials, too, benefited from his expansion of Caesar's policies, so that Roman citizenship was for many a realistic goal, and the fear of rapacious officials was significantly lessened. With an emphasis on provincial prosperity and stability, armies could be kept to a size that was politically and economically acceptable: they certainly did not approach the huge numbers of which the triumvirs had disposed. This, in its turn, served to push into the background the ultimate military sanction that was, of course, his. It was important, too, that the army was made permanent, with regular terms of service, leading to a retirement that was funded initially by Augustus himself, but subsequently from taxation. This permanent army was stationed not near Rome, but in the provinces where it was needed.

Augustus recognised also that the *respublica* did not consist simply of a set of political institutions: family life, traditional religious practices, the agricultural stability of the Italian small farmer – all came within the orbit of his patronal care. He was *pater patriae*, the national 'father-figure', the guarantor of peace, stability and the gods' continuing favour. After nearly half a century in power, Augustus by the end of his life was seen as indispensable to the continued well-being of the *respublica* – in many ways, a Ciceronian *moderator*.

The weakness of the Augustan system proved to be the manner in which he tried to secure its stability in the long term. Whilst in theory members of the senatorial nobility could aspire to a primacy like his, they lacked in practice the means to achieve it during his lifetime. Realising perhaps the dangers that threatened in a revival of factional squabbling amongst the nobility, including the type that had characterised his own triumviral relationship with Antonius, Augustus determined that the future should be secured within a dynastic framework, based upon his and Livia's families – the *Julii* and the *Claudii*.

The historian Tacitus saw this as the return of *dominatio*, and the later emperor Galba observed that the fact that Rome had in effect become the heirloom of Augustus' family represented an attack upon *libertas*. Whilst nobody would doubt the great capabilities of Augustus himself, the necessary blend of qualities was by no means obvious in Tiberius (AD 14–37), Caligula (AD 37–41), Claudius (AD 41–54) or Nero (AD 54–68). Their weaknesses, and particularly their inability to step directly into the shoes of Augustus, served to show that the dynastic approach required modification, and a way needed to be found by which *principatus* and *libertas* could be harmonised. Thus, by the end of the first century AD, in a manner that recalled the republic, every office, including the role of *princeps*, was open to any senator by the consensus of his peers.

However, despite the changes that occurred in the century after Augustus, his successors continued to see him as the ultimate source of their authority and as representing the standard by which they would be judged. Augustus' acknowledged success, both during his lifetime and subsequently, demonstrates how wrong Antonius had been when he dismissed

Octavian as owing everything to his name: although it may have been unintentional, Cicero was nearer the mark in seeing Octavian as 'the divine youth', for it was he who in the *pax Augusta* guaranteed the survival of the Roman *respublica*.

Appendix I

Roman voting assemblies

	Comitia curiata	*Comitia centuriata*	*Comitia tributa*	*Concilium plebis*
Composition				
voting units	30 curiae, 10 each from 3 ancient tribes	193 centuries – 18 cavalry, 170 infantry (arranged in the ratio 80, 20, 20, 20, 30, according to 5 property classes), 5 of unarmed (i.e. unpropertied) citizens	35 tribes	35 tribes
citizens attending	each curia represented by one man (a lictor)	all citizens	all citizens	plebeians only
presiding officer	consul or praetor or (for religious purposes) chief priest	consul or praetor	consul or praetor or curule aedile	tribune of the plebs or plebeian aedile
Duties				
elections		consuls, praetors, censors	curule aediles, quaestors, lower officers, special commissioners	tribunes and aediles of the plebs
legislative	confirmed *imperium* of magistrates; confirmed adoptions and wills	(until about 218 BC, chief law-making body); subsequently used for declaration of war, confirmation of powers of censors	all types except those restricted to *comitia centuriata*	all types except those restricted to *comitia centuriata*; decisions (known as *plebiscita*) had force of law after 287 BC
judicial		capital charges (increasingly after 150 BC limited to treason-charges)	all crimes against the state which were punishable by fine; (after the time of the Gracchi, these duties increasingly lost to the other courts)	

Appendix II
Magistracies of the Roman republic

Consul Two **consuls** elected annually by the *comitia centuriata*; both had *imperium* (executive power), and were recognised as the chief military and political executives of the state, the tenure of the **consulship** generally being regarded as the apex of a political career (save perhaps for the censorship). The **consuls** would command armies in the field, preside over the *comitia* and the senate, and they proposed laws to the people (*ius agendi cum populo*). They theoretically had rights of jurisdiction, though in criminal cases this was generally delegated, and civil jurisdiction was taken over by the **praetor urbanus**. Each was attended by twelve lictors. (After 367 BC, at least one consul had to be a plebeian.)

Praetor The office went back probably to the regal period, though it appears to have been 're-invented', probably in 367 BC, and possibly as a way of answering the concession of that year which gave one of the annual **consulships** as of right to a plebeian. A **praetor** was elected each year with special responsibility for civil jurisdiction (**praetor urbanus**): but he, and his later colleagues, possessed *imperium* and could properly act as army commanders and preside over the assemblies and senate and introduce business to them. The **praetor's** *imperium*, however, was inferior to that of the **consul** and had to yield before it, and he was attended by only six lictors. In 242 BC, a second

praetor was added to deal with civil jurisdiction between citizens and foreigners (**praetor peregrinus**). Two further **praetors** were instituted in 227 BC with responsibility respectively for Sicily and Sardinia, so that there were four **praetors** elected annually by the beginning of the second Punic War. Two more were instituted in 197 BC to govern the two provinces of Spain, and the number was raised to eight by Sulla and to sixteen by Julius Caesar. **Praetors** were elected in the *comitia centuriata*.

The **praetor urbanus** had the duty of publishing an *edict* stating the principles according to which he proposed to administer justice, and these edicts were the cumulative source of much Roman law in later times.

The **consulship** and the **praetorship** were the only two regular magistracies that carried *imperium*; but there was provision for the *imperium* of a **consul** or **praetor** to be prolonged (*prorogatio*), and, in later times, certainly from Sulla onwards, it was in virtue of such prolonged *imperium* that ex-**consuls** and ex-**praetors** (known as *proconsuls* and *propraetors*) governed provinces. It also sometimes happened that a special grant of *imperium*, specified as consular, praetorian or proconsular might be conferred on a named individual (as with Scipio Africanus in 210 BC, and more notably with Augustus after 31 BC).

Dictator   There was provision in an emergency for a **consul** to nominate a **dictator** with overriding *imperium*, who was to hold office only for six months or for the duration of the emergency, whichever was the shorter; a **dictator** was attended by twenty-four lictors. (According to these rules the dictatorship of Sulla and most of Caesar's tenures of the office in the 40s BC were irregular.)

The **dictator** in addition had the right to appoint his deputy, the *Master of the Horse*, and to delegate his *imperium* to him – the only instance according to regular procedure of a holder of *imperium* being allowed to delegate that *imperium* to another without reference to the people; the practice was extended when Pompey (who was never **dictator**) was allowed in 67 BC and also in 55 BC to appoint deputies with *imperium*, and when Augustus was allowed to appoint his own deputies to govern provinces.

Censor   Two elected by *comitia centuriata*, generally every five years, holding office only until their functions were performed, and anyway for not more than eighteen months. Their primary task was to revise the list of citizens, ensure their proper registration, and assess the value of their property and their 'moral worth'. To this was added a review of the membership of the senate in which they could enrol new members, and remove any who seemed morally unworthy. A **censor** could not be called to account for his actions as **censor**. Although the office did not carry *imperium*, it was regarded as the most august of magistracies, and its holders were almost always ex-**consuls**.

Aedile Four elected annually, of whom two were 'curule' aediles, two 'plebeian' aediles. Strictly only the **curule aediles** were magistrates, elected by the *comitia tributa*, the **plebeian aediles** being elected by the plebs alone, in the *concilium plebis*. The functions of the two kinds of **aediles** were, however, apparently indistinguishable. They had a general responsibility for maintenance in the city of Rome, a *cura urbis* (maintaining roads, water supply, etc.), a responsibility to maintain the corn supply (*cura annonae*), and they were expected to lay on magnificent games. They also had some limited powers of jurisdiction in minor matters.

Quaestor The most junior magistracy; originally two were appointed by the **consuls** as their assistants. The number was increased to four and made subject to election, traditionally in 421 BC. From about 267 BC, there were eight **quaestors**, until Sulla increased the number to twenty. Of the eight in office in the third and second centuries BC, two were **quaestores urbani**, to whom were delegated the conduct of murder trials, whilst two were expected to assist the **consul** in the field. They clearly had financial responsibilities. Elected by the *comitia tributa*, ex-**quaestors** automatically (after Sulla) became members of the senate.

Plebeian offices

Tribune of the plebs Ten elected annually; they had sacrosanctity (personal inviolability), the right and duty of bringing help to a citizen being arrested by a magistrate (*ius auxilii ferendi*), the right to veto the action of a magistrate, thus for instance stopping the levy or stopping a motion being put to the vote of the senate or *comitia*, and the right to convene and put proposals to the *concilium plebis*, whose resolutions (*plebiscita*), at least after 287 BC, had the force of law. Thus, in effect, they had the right to propose laws. (Sulla tried to restrict the tribunate's effectiveness by preventing its holders from proceeding to further office.)

Plebeian aedile   See under **aediles**.

Cursus honorum (sequence of offices)

The usual order of offices for a politically ambitious person was: **quaestor** (probably at minimum age of about 28); **aedile** or **tribune of the plebs; praetor; consul**. Two-year gaps were required between offices, though it seems that the aedileship/tribunate could be missed out. The age requirements were stiffened by Sulla as follows: **quaestor**, 30; **praetor**, 39; **Consul**, 42. It was further enacted by Sulla that not more than one magistracy could be held at a time by the same man; nor could a man hold the same office twice within a ten-year period (both rules being broken by Sulla himself).

Appendix III
The provinces of the Roman empire

Provinces and dates of acquisition

BC	241	Sicily
	238	Sardinia; Corsica
	198	Hispania Tarraconensis and Baetica
	146	Africa
		Macedonia
	133	Asia
	121	Transalpine Gaul
	100(?)	Cilicia
	89	Cisalpine Gaul (northern Italy)
	74	Cyrene
	67	Crete
	63	Bithynia-Pontus
		Syria
	58	Cyprus
	53(?)	Dalmatia
	51	Gallia Lugdunensis
		Gallia Belgica

————————————————————————————Battle of Actium

	30	Egypt
	27	Aquitania
		Achaea
	25	Galatia

	16	Lusitania
	15	Raetia
		Noricum
	14	Cottian Alps
		Maritime Alps
AD	6	Moesia
		Judaea
	10	Pannonia
	12	Germania Superior
		Germania Inferior
	17	Commagene
		Cappadocia
	40	Mauretania Caesariensis
		Mauretania Tingitana
	43	Britain
		Lycia
		Thrace
	106	Dacia
		Arabia
	114	Armenia
	115	Mesopotamia
		Parthia

Appendix IV
Principal dates

BC   753 Foundation of Rome by Romulus (trad.)

753–509 Regal period (trad.)

509 Expulsion of Tarquinius Superbus; establishment of the republic (trad.)

494 Introduction of office of tribune of the plebs (trad.)

421 Quaestorship (and thus senatorial membership) opened to plebeians

367 Enactment that one consul each year should be a plebeian

339 Publilian law enacts sovereignty of the plebeian assembly

287 Hortensian law re-enacts the provision of the Publilian law

264–241 First Punic War; acquisition of first overseas provinces

218–202 Second Punic War; Hannibal's invasion of Italy

146 Destruction of Carthage and Corinth

145 (or 140?) Abortive land bill of Scipio's faction

137 Numantine War; Tiberius Gracchus' rupturing of relations with Scipio Aemilianus

133 Tribunate and death of Tiberius Gracchus

131 Italian 'cause' espoused by Aemilianus

129 Death (murder?) of Scipio Aemilianus

126 Expulsion of Italians from Rome
125 Abortive franchise bill of Fulvius Flaccus; revolt of Fregellae
123–122 Tribunates of Gaius Gracchus
121 Suicide of Gaius Gracchus
118 Outbreak of war in north Africa against Jugurtha
109 Metellus Numidicus in north Africa
107 Marius' first consulship; takes over conduct of the African War
105 Defeat of Jugurtha
102–101 Marius' fourth and fifth consulships; defeats inflicted on the Cimbri and Teutones
100 Marius' sixth consulship; *senatus consultum ultimum* passed against Saturninus and Glaucia
98 Caecilian-Didian law passed to prevent 'omnibus' legislation
95 Expulsion of Italians from Rome
91 Tribunate and death of Marcus Livius Drusus
91–88 Social War
88 Sulla's first consulship; legislation of Sulpicius Rufus; Sulla's first march on Rome
87–83 Sulla in the east; war against Mithridates
87 Massacre of *optimates* at the hands of the Marians
86 Marius' seventh consulship
82 Sulla's second march on Rome
81–79 Sulla's dictatorship and constitutional reforms; proscription programme
79 Sulla's resignation
77 Pompey puts down revolt of Lepidus
77–73 Pompey in Spain
73–71 Revolt of Spartacus; return of Pompey
70 Joint consulship of Pompey and Crassus; dismantling of Sulla's constitution
67 Gabinian law gives Pompey the command against the pirates
66 Manilian law gives Pompey the command against Mithridates
65 So-called 'first Catilinarian conspiracy'

63 Consulship of Cicero; abortive legislation of Rullus; Catilinarian conspiracy; death of Mithridates

62 Pompey's return from the east; Clodius and the *Bona Dea* affair

60 Formation of first triumvirate of Pompey, Crassus and Caesar

59 Caesar's first consulship; Clodius' transfer to the plebs

58 Tribunate of Clodius, banishment of Cicero

58–49 Caesar in Gaul

57 Recall of Cicero from exile; Pompey's corn commission

56 Gang warfare in Rome; renewal of the triumvirate at Lucca

55 Second joint consulship of Pompey and Crassus

54 Death of Julia

53 Death of Crassus at Carrhae; Pompey's marriage to Cornelia

52 Murder of Clodius; anarchy in Rome; Pompey appointed 'sole consul'

50 Discussion of Caesar's position in Gaul; tribunate of Curio

49 Caesar's crossing of the Rubicon

49–45 Civil war

48 Defeat of Pompey at Pharsalus; murdered later in Egypt

46 Suicide of Cato

44 Caesar made *dictator perpetuus*; murder of Caesar (Ides of March)

43 Second triumvirate of Antonius, Octavian and Lepidus; proscription of Cicero

42 Battle of Philippi; suicides of Brutus and Cassius

41–40 Perusine War against Lucius Antonius

40 Treaty of Brundisium patching up second triumvirate

39 Treaty of Misenum with Sextus Pompeius; return of republican 'exiles'

38 Octavian's marriage to Livia

37 Treaty of Tarentum; renewal of the second triumvirate

36	Defeat and death of Sextus Pompeius; disgrace of Lepidus
36–32	Preparations for war between Octavian and Antonius
34	'Donations of Alexandria'
31	Battle of Actium
30	Suicides of Antonius and Cleopatra
27	First settlement of the Augustan *principate*
23	Second settlement of the Augustan *principate*
AD 14	Death and deification of Augustus; accession of Tiberius as the first Julio-Claudian successor

Further reading

Primary sources

Some of our information comes from later classical authors; of these, the most significant is Plutarch (*c.* AD 120), whose Roman biographies are collected in two volumes in Penguin Classics – *Makers of Rome* and *The Fall of the Roman Republic*. Besides Plutarch, considerable use is made of the historical writings of Appian (*c.* AD 150), Dio Cassius (*c.* AD 220) and of Suetonius' *Life of Caesar* (*c.* AD 120). These are, of course, in various ways dependent upon earlier authors, some of whom survive in fragmentary form. It is clear, however, that whilst the late republic could be an attractive subject for early imperial writers, it could also be one that tested the sensibilities of Augustus' successors; Cremutius Cordus, writing during the reign of Tiberius, was prosecuted for praising Brutus and Cassius. Perhaps the greatest loss amongst authors of this kind is represented by the later books of Augustus' friend, the historian Livy, to whom Augustus is said to have referred as 'my Pompeian friend'.

Much contemporary or near-contemporary writing survives and is available in Penguin Classics; these include many of Cicero's forensic and political speeches, though we have to bear in mind that the published versions usually represent Cicero's own later 'working-up' of the originals, so that what survives may be what he would have liked to have said rather than what he did say; his surviving speech in defence of Titus Annius Milo (on trial for the murder of Clodius) is a celebrated example of this. Most importantly, a very large collection of Cicero's *Letters* survives, and is available in Penguin Classics. The collection was put together after Cicero's death by his former slave, Tiro, and *may* have been subject to some censorship by Octavian and Antonius. A selection of Ciceronian passages relating to the management of the republic is translated by W.K. Lacey and B.W.J. Wilson in *Res Publica*, Oxford 1970. Caesar's accounts of the *Gallic War* and the *Civil War* are available, as are Sallust's monographs on the *Jugurthine War* and the *Catilinarian Conspiracy*. Sallust's *Histories*, however, survive only as fragments.

Modern authors

The problems of the late republic have given rise to a very large bibliography of books and articles. The best general works are:

Cambridge Ancient History, vol. IX, Cambridge 1932
M.H. Crawford *The Roman Republic*, London 1978
H.H. Scullard *From the Gracchi to Nero*, London 1962

Of the studies of particular themes, personalities and problems in the period, the following may be consulted:

F.E. Adcock *Marcus Crassus, Millionaire*, Cambridge 1966
A.E. Astin *Scipio Aemilianus*, Oxford 1967
P.A. Brunt *Social Conflicts in the Roman Republic*, London 1971
T.F. Carney *A Biography of Gaius Marius*, Chicago 1970
B. Caven *The Punic Wars*, London 1980
M.L. Clarke *The Noblest Roman: Marcus Brutus and his Reputation*, London 1981
D.C. Earl *Tiberius Gracchus: A Study in Politics*, Brussels 1963
D.C. Earl *The Moral and Political Tradition of Rome*, London 1967
M. Gelzer *Caesar: Politician and Statesman*, Oxford 1968
M. Gelzer *The Roman Nobility*, Oxford 1969
E. Gjerstad *Legends and Facts of Early Rome*, Lund 1960
P. Greenhalgh *Pompey*, London, two vols, 1980 and 1981
K. Hopkins *Conquerors and Slaves*, Cambridge 1978

E. Huzar *Mark Antony: A Biography*, Minnesota 1978

A. Keaveney *Sulla: The Last Republican*, London 1982

A. Keaveney *Lucullus: A Life*, London 1992

A.W. Lintott *Violence in Republican Rome*, Oxford 1968

C.L. Nicolet *The World of the Citizen in Republican Rome*, London 1980

H.H. Scullard *A History of the Roman World from 753 to 146 B.C.*, London 1960

R. Seager (ed.) *The Crisis of the Roman Republic*, Cambridge 1969

R. Seager *Pompey: A Political Biography*, Oxford 1979

D.C.A. Shotter *Augustus Caesar*, London 1991

D.L. Stockton *Cicero: A Political Biography*, Oxford 1971

D.L. Stockton *The Gracchi*, Oxford 1979

R. Syme *The Roman Revolution*, Oxford 1939

R. Syme *Sallust*, Cambridge 1964

L.R. Taylor *Party Politics in the Age of Caesar*, Berkeley 1949

C. Wirszubski *Libertas as a Political Idea at Rome*, Cambridge 1950

Z. Yavetz *Plebs and Princeps*, Oxford 1969

A complete listing of the magistrates of the republic may be found in T.R.S. Broughton *The Magistrates of the Roman Republic*, New York 1952.